7 LAYERS OF CONVERSATION

Seven Manifestations of the Holy Spirit

PATRICIA A. MORGAN

7 LAYERS OF CONVERSATION
SEVEN MANIFESTATIONS OF THE HOLY SPIRIT

iUniverse books may be ordered through booksellers or by contacting:

iUniverse
1663 Liberty Drive
Bloomington, IN 47403
www.iuniverse.com
844-349-9409

ISBN: 978-1-6632-5178-7 (sc)
ISBN: 978-1-6632-5179-4 (e)

Library of Congress Control Number: 2023905600

Print information available on the last page.

iUniverse rev. date: 06/26/2023

To my mother, Ruby Mitchell Glover
and in memory of my father, James Bennett

CONTENTS

Walking with the Spirit

Let's begin this journey by walking down the seven streets of the manifestation of the Holy Spirit. He is all encompassing, and to him there is no end or measure. In writing this book, I am truly excited to present my best friend, the Holy Spirit, to those of the faith and to introduce him to others perhaps for the first time. If you are reading this book, you were drawn, I can say truly, by the Spirit of God. The world may not know him, but we who are of the faith do—or should.

The Spirit of God begin to compel me to begin to write this book over Labor Day weekend, 2022, when so many people were traveling, barbecuing, and having what they call fun. I had just gotten over one of the most challenging times I'd had to endure in a long while. Suddenly I knew that I could just put pen to paper. I began to write the vision, made a plan, and ran with it.

Even as I am writing this preface to you now, I can feel the Spirit of God upon me, giving me the strength and agility to write as I hear the raindrops outside my window. I am prepared to go as deep as the Holy Spirit would like in revealing himself in the pages of this book.

We should acknowledge that we will never know everything about him, for we know in part and we prophesy in part. But he has laid the foundation whereupon we can live a successful life through knowing him. And yes, he is a person, not a thing. If you get to know him, you will ask yourself, "What took me so long to find this wonderful person who resides inside of me, the gift my Savior left me?" I can see why Jesus said it was expedient that he go away so that the Holy Spirit should come. What a wonderful gift he left his children! He knew we would need the fullness of his Spirit to do this thing call life.

I am not coming to you in the pages of a book as if you don't know who the Holy Spirit is—you may or may not—but I'm coming in the volume of this book to introduce to you the manifestations of the Spirit.

The words are leaping off my heart to fill the pages. What I love about the Holy Spirit is that we all are his friends. He is not biased or prejudiced, nor does he prefer one over the other. He loves us all the same, and—here comes the shocker—even if we don't love him in return, it doesn't change his mind about you. He loves you first before you love him.

ACKNOWLEDGMENTS

I have dedicated this book to my mother, Ruby Mitchell Glover, who is alive and striving. She is one of, if not *the* strongest, most self-willed person I know. I know that my family and friends would agree. She and my father, James Bennett, who has transitioned to be with the Lord, taught me the ways of the Lord at a very young age.

My dad was a little more radical than my mom—I know that is where I get my Jesus fanatic ways. (Any friend or family member reading this book is probably shaking their head and laughing out loud at that.)

My parents didn't have much in material things to give me and my siblings, but they gave us the best inheritance in the world, and that is the Word of God.

Mapping Seven Manifestations of the Holy Spirit

The Bible does not say there are Seven Spirits of God. However, it does talk about seven manifestations of the Spirit. In my studies, I have found that the number 7 in Hebrew is a sacred number or a holy number. It symbolizes perfection, fullness, abundance, rest, grace, and completion.

The seven manifestations of the Spirit of God represent the fullness of the Holy Spirit, which is freely given to us— nothing we had to pay for, as Christ left us this gift. It was so wonderful he emphasized that it was expedient for him to leave.

We are not given the Spirt in measure, but we were given all of God's best in fullness when we receive Christ as our savior. This may be hard for many to comprehend. Most of us have seen only a few of the manifestations of the Holy Spirit. In this book, we will dive deeply and bring out those hidden areas that may have been gray for you. My hope for you is that after reading this book you will be stirred up, and regain new confidence and boldness to pursue the things of God with the help of the Holy Spirit.

The *Ruach* without Measure

When the Spirit of God (*ruach*) came upon Daniel, Esther, Samson, and all of God's prophets, priests, judges, kings, and rulers of old, they received the anointing in measure. The Bible says of Jesus, "for he whom God hath sent speaketh the words of God: for God giveth him not the Spirit by measure unto him" (John 3:34).* That tells me Jesus had the fullness of God without measure, and so do we.

Now, that's good news if we ever needed it. That is why Jesus, before he departed this earth, said to his disciples, "As my Father hath sent me, even so send I you" (John 20:2). In other words, Jesus was imparting into them the fullness of God without measure.

Thank God, we are joint heirs with Christ Jesus, according to Romans 8:17. That means we have the same anointing without measure as Jesus, our brother.

The Seven Spirits

> And there shall come forth a rod out of the stem of Jesse and a branch shall grow out of his roots: And the spirit of the Lord shall rest upon him, the spirit of wisdom and understanding, the spirit of counsel and might, the spirit of knowledge and the fear of the Lord; And shall make him of quick understanding in the fear of the Lord: and

---

* Unless otherwise noted, all quotations from the Bible come from the King James Version.

he shall not judge after the sight of his eyes,
neither reprove after the hearing of his ears:
But with righteousness shall he judge the
poor, and reprove with equity for the meek
of the earth.

These are the words from the prophet Isaiah, who prophesied Jesus would come from the stem of Jesse, the father of David. Therefore, Jesus described himself as the root and offspring of David in Revelation 22:16. He is the root from which David came forth, but in his earthly nature he comes from David's lineage as his offspring. We know through the gospels he was spoken of as the Son of David.

Isaiah spoke also about how he would be quick of understanding and the fear of the Lord (Isaiah 11:3–4).

And the spirit of the Lord shall rest
upon him, the spirit of wisdom and
understanding, the spirit of counsel and
might, the spirit of knowledge and of the
fear of the Lord. (Isaiah 11:2)

This passage lists seven distinct Spirits:

1. The Spirit of the Lord
2. The Spirit of Wisdom
3. The Spirit of Understanding
4. The Spirit of Counsel
5. The Spirit of Might
6. The Spirit of Knowledge
7. The Spirit of the Fear of the Lord

The scriptures elsewhere speak about the seven spirits variously as the seven eyes, the seven Spirits, or the seven lamps, particularly in the book of Revelation.

> John to the seven churches which are in Asia: Grace be unto you and peace, from him which is, and which was and which is to come; and from the seven Spirits which are before his throne. (Revelation 1:4)

This verse refers to the seven separate and independent manifestations of the Holy Spirit in the life of the believer, which is indicative of the fullness of the Spirit of God.

> And out of the throne proceeded lightnings and thundering and voices: and there were seven lamps of fire burning before the throne, which are the seven Spirits of God. (Revelation 4:5)

I can truly say there is nothing we have seen on this planet that can come close to what we are reading, but the good news is that we will see it one day, and I don't believe it is far off.

> And I beheld and lo, in the midst of the throne and of the four beasts, and in the midst of the elders, stood a Lamb as it had been slain, having seven horns and seven eyes, which are the seven Spirits of God send forth into all the earth. (Revelation 5:6)

This scripture lets us know that God sees everything; nothing is hidden from him. That is why David said in Psalm 139:8, "If I ascend to heaven, you are there, If I make my bed in hell, behold, thou are there."

The Seven Spirits of God are seven independent manifestations of the Holy Spirit. This is distinct from the Godhead as a phenomenon, which is made up of three persons—Father, Son, and Holy Spirit—each having a distinct personality with different characteristics and attributes. It would take a lifetime to scratch the surface of our incredible God!

The prophet Zechariah also talks about the seven Spirits:

> For behold the stone that I have laid before Joshua; upon one stone shall seven eyes; behold, I will engrave the graving thereof, saith the Lord of hosts and I will remove the iniquity of that land in one day. Upon on stone shall be seven eyes. (Zechariah 3:9)

> For who hath despised the day of small things? For they shall rejoice and shall see the plummet in the hand of Zerubbabel with those seven; they are the eyes of the Lord which run to and for through the whole earth. (Zechariah 4:10)

To which I would compare Revelation 5:6:

> And I beheld, and lo in the midst of the throne and of the four beasts, and in the midst of the elders, stood a Lamb as it had

been slain, having seven horns and seven eyes, which are the seven Spirits of God sent forth into all the earth.

All the above scriptures speak as one about the Seven Spirits of God and the fullness of Holy Spirit and how He operates in his kingdom where there is no end.

The Seven-Eyed Stone

If so be ye have tasted that the Lord is gracious. To whom coming, as unto a living stone, disallowed indeed of men, but chose of God, and precious, Ye also a lively stone, are built up a spiritual house, and holy priesthood, to offer up spiritual sacrifices, acceptable to God by Jesus Christ. Wherefore also it is contained in the scripture, Behold, I lay in Zion a chief corner stone, elect, precious: and he that believeth on him shall not be confounded. (1 Peter 2:3–6)

Jesus is the Stone that Peter was talking about, and we are also the living stones formed and fashioned after him. Recall that Zechariah said, "Upon one stone shall be seven eyes." He did not say upon *the* stone, but upon *one* stone—in other words, there are other stones, which are the seven eyes of the Spirit of God.

Street Name –
The Spirit of the Lord

And the spirit of the Lord shall rest upon him.
Isaiah 11:2

The first of the seven Spirits listed by the prophet Isaiah represents the Spirit of dominion and Lordship. Sadly, many Christians know little or nothing about the Holy Spirit, the one who rests upon you or comes upon you and anoints you to do the work of the Father. He is the one that helps you deliver the Word to your congregation or your brother or sister in Christ. He anoints you with power to carry out the will of the Father. On your own, you can do nothing. The flesh is weak, but the Spirit is willing always.

There will not be a time in your life that the Holy Spirit will get tired. He is the one that gives you the boldness and courage needed for the journey. He puts you ahead of any situation or circumstance you may face. As we know from the scriptures, whenever the prophets stood to declare God's

Word, they did not stand as mere men but with boldness and power because the Spirit of the Lord came upon them to assist with the assignment at hand.

The Spirit of the Lord is the reason Esther said, "If I perish, I perish" (Esther 4:16). The Holy Spirit also assisted Daniel when he went before King Nebuchadnezzar to deliver the word of the Lord.

> During the night, the mystery was revealed to Daniel in a vision. Then Daniel praised the God of heaven and said:
>
> "Praise be to the name of God for ever and ever; wisdom and power are his.
> He changes times and seasons; he deposes kings and raises up others.
> He gives wisdom to the wise and knowledge to the discerning.
> He reveals deep and hidden things: he knows what lies in darkness, and light dwells with him.
> I thank and praise you, God of my ancestors: You have given me wisdom and power, you have made known to me what we asked of you, you have made known to us the dream of the king." (Daniel 2:19–23 NIV)

When God's Spirit rests upon you, there is nothing that is impossible for you to accomplish. For we know that God has not given us the spirit of fear (or timidity) but of power and love and of a sound mind (2 Timothy 1:7).

When the Spirit of God comes upon you, he is also able

to transport you without a passport, just as he did Philip in
Acts 8:39:

> And when they were come up out of the
> water; the Spirit of the Lord caught away
> Phillip, that the eunuch saw him no more
> and he went on his way rejoicing.

The Spirit of the Lord empowers you: "You shall receive
power; after the Holy Spirit is come upon you; and you shall
be witnesses unto me both in Jerusalem, and in all Judea
and in Samaria, and the uttermost part of the earth" (Acts
1:8). Before this time, he had told them to wait in the city of
Jerusalem "until you be endued with power from on high."
This is the highlight of the beginning of Pentecost when the
Holy Spirit came upon them.

When the Holy Spirit empowers you, a surge of energy
comes upon you that you cannot explain. You have no word
to articulate it; you just flow with it and let the Holy Spirit
do the work through you that could never get done in your
own strength. I call this *dunamis* power!

Imagine for a moment the day when Pentecost came.
On this day, many were gathered on one accord, waiting
and expecting, as they were instructed, to see the move
of the Holy Spirit. They were not disappointed. He came
upon them with power and authority. They were able to
preach supernaturally and teach the Word of God. The
Bible says they were clothed with supernatural power; to
me, this sounds like an invisible power that wrapped himself
around everyone. They were all filled with the Spirit without
measure, and many were saved that day. This is all a part

of God's plan that his children know the mysteries of the kingdom.

The same Spirit that was upon Jesus is upon us:

> The Spirit of the Lord is upon me, because he hath anointed me to preach the gospel to the poor; he hath sent me to heal the brokenhearted, to preach deliverance to the captives, and recovering of sight to the blind, to set at liberty them that are bruised, to preach the acceptable year of the Lord. (Luke 4:18–19)

The Holy Spirit is a person of the Trinity and wants to be revered and known by each of God's children. He longs for fellowship and to guide you through this life we have been given.

I lived in New Jersey for a good part of my life, before I really knew who the Holy Spirit was. He spoke to me one day and told me he would be whatever I needed him to be to me—guide, nutritionist, friend, counselor, life coach . . .. I am inviting you to let the Holy Spirit be to you whatever you need him to be. This is not to discount those who may be in one of the professions I listed or in any other profession, but at the end of the day, he is the greatest teacher of this life, and God knows we need all the help we can get. I am asking you to please continue the work God has gifted you to flow in.

If you are looking to the world for answers, please stop today: you will never find it. All that is in this world is the lust of the flesh, the lust of the eyes, and the pride of life (1 John 2:16). The true source is the Holy Spirit.

Get Stirred Up!

By this point, you may be wondering how to get your power back. It's not just about teaching, preaching, singing, praying, or prophesying—it's about *demonstration*.

People are searching for the move of God. They want to see the demonstration of the Spirit and of power. Sometimes they try New Age or other forms of spirituality but deny the true power that has entered the world. Your faith shouldn't stand in the wisdom of men but in the power of God (1 Corinthians 2:4). I beseech you to embark on the power that was left for you. Get to know the Holy Spirit as truly yours.

CHAPTER 2

Street Name —
The Spirit of Wisdom

And the spirit of the Lord shall rest upon him,
the spirit of wisdom.

Isaiah 11:2

Wisdom is another manifestation of the Holy Spirt. Who doesn't need wisdom during the times we are living in? These are critical days, hours, minutes, seconds when we must hear what the Spirit is saying. We can no longer go our way as if there is no accountability to the one that gave his life and the gift of the Holy Spirit to us. We must acknowledge him in all the ways that he directs our path.

In Ephesians 1:17, Paul asked "that the God of our Lord Jesus Christ, the Father of glory, may give unto you the spirit of wisdom and revelation in the knowledge of him." Paul saw that the Ephesian Christians were on point when it came to the power and glory of God but lacked wisdom and revelation knowledge.

I can attest to the same thing happening today in the body of Christ. It's time to get back to the old landmarks and to seek the wisdom of God. God's people are some of the most gifted people on the planet. They have the gifts of the Spirit; they can prophesy and have great things happen; they sing, dance, teach, preach, and so on. But when it comes to walking in God's wisdom, there is such a great lack. It's time for us as the body of Christ to do better and to ask the Holy Spirit for his wisdom and knowledge, so that we are a balanced people not wanting for anything.

The street we should be walking on is called Wisdom. You may have heard wisdom described as the ability to apply knowledge that has been obtained. Well, I'm here to tell you that real wisdom can come only from the Holy Spirit functioning in you to make sure all your decisions are sound. Wisdom gives you the advantage in life that most will never have because they don't have a relationship with the Holy Spirt. Wisdom is such a force! It will tell you when to move, and when not to move; when to sell, and when not to sell; when to buy, and when not to buy; when to hold, and when to fold; when to keep to it, and when to let go.

So many people—and I'm including myself—have a fear of making the wrong decisions. We all deal with it. It's the human side of us. That is why it's so imperative that we commune with the Holy Spirit. Go to him first, not to your parents, spouse, siblings, or anyone else. See what Wisdom would say concerning the matter first. You will make the right decision, and it will save you from grief and pain.

Now that's good news! Apply wisdom and let the Holy Spirit guide you. You should still be excited! Let's continue on the street called Wisdom.

Prudence and Knowledge

> I wisdom dwell with prudence, and
> find out knowledge of witty inventions.
> (Proverbs 8:12)

This verse tells me that there is one greater than Elon Musk, the sometime-richest man in the world. What if you seek the one that can give you a "witty invention" overnight? One that will catapult your entire family and generations into their God-given destiny? Now that's worth seeking out.

Some of you stay up all night and think about what you can do to move yourself along with your family into a better situation. But there is an inner struggle because you are not asking the one who has the answers. Ask Wisdom, and you will not be disappointed.

The great thing about Wisdom—it doesn't travel alone. There is Prudence, which gives you the ability to discern in your everyday affairs. You gain the advantage of insight and foresight. With Wisdom, you've got it made!

When Wisdom has full control of your life, there is no need to worry about the cares of this life, as most do—what we will eat and drink, what clothes we will wear, how to endure sickness and disease or anything that is contrary to the Word of God. You will be in such peace that it will pass the understanding of men. They will marvel and ask you how you can be in such peace in times like this. That is your opportunity to introduce the Spirit of Wisdom.

Getting to Know Wisdom

> She [Wisdom] is more precious than rubies and all the things thou canst desire are not to be compared unto her. Length of days is in her right hand, and in her left-hand riches and honor. Her ways are ways of pleasantness, and all her paths are peace. (Proverbs: 3:15–17)

> But of him [God] are ye in Christ Jesus who of God is made unto us wisdom, and righteousness, and sanctification and redemption. (1 Corinthians 1:30)

The New Testament tells us that we have something Solomon in all his wisdom didn't have: Christ. He's our wisdom "in whom are hid all the treasures of wisdom and knowledge" (Colossians 2:3). In other words, he is the embodiment of all wisdom and knowledge. Making him your Lord and Savior comes with a benefits package.

Those who are in a corporate setting may seek out the benefits even more than the pay. If you are experienced, you know that the benefits can outweigh the pay and will sustain you and your family until the assignment is completed. It's the same in our relationship with Christ: God's benefits will sustain us through this life assignment until he calls us home. That's why Psalm 103:2 reminds us not to forget his benefits.

"It is the glory of God to conceal a thing: but the honor of kings is to search out a matter," Proverbs 25:2 notes. This is what the Bible calls the holy knowledge of

God. God hides it from the world; only his children really know what time it is. He ministers his divine wisdom to your mind by the anointing of the Holy Spirit, and you began this journey of discovering the secret things of God.

If you are not in "the God club," then please join us! The only thing you need to do is accept him as your Lord and Savior, and all these things will be added unto you.

Let God Celebrate You!

As you continue on the street named Wisdom, you will learn that it can be not only seen but also heard.

> And the spirit of the Lord shall rest upon him [and] the spirit of wisdom … and shall make him of quick understanding in the fear of the LORD: and he shall not judge after the sight of his eyes, neither reprove after the hearing of his ear. (Isaiah 11:2–3)

A great example of wisdom being seen and heard is when Mary, the mother of Jesus, instructs the servants at the wedding at Cana to "do whatever he tells you" (John 2:5). She did not doubt, and when Jesus told them to fill the water pots, they did as instructed. The best wine was poured and saved for last. Because of the wisdom of God, they were able to continue to enjoy the wedding without any mishaps. I believe the wedding was better later on than at the beginning. What a celebration!

Now that you have read this chapter, go before God

and ask the Holy Spirit to let the manifestation of wisdom and prudence begin to flow in your life. I promise that by the end of this book, you can be walking in all seven manifestations of the Holy Spirit.

CHAPTER 3

Street Name –
The Spirit of Understanding

That the God of our Lord Jesus Christ, the
Father of glory, may give unto you the spirit
of wisdom and revelation in the knowledge
of him: The eyes of your understanding being
enlightened; that ye may know what the hope
of his calling is and what the riches of the glory
of the inheritance in the saints.

Ephesians 1:17–18

"The eyes of your understanding being enlightened" is
the operation of the Spirit of understanding. He helps you
understand your God-given calling, what you were created
to do on the earth. In other words, he assists you with
fulfilling the call of God on your life and the wealth of His
glorious inheritance in you. He guides you and shows you
the way and the mandate that is placed upon you.

Today, many may have the manifestations of Spirit but

lack understanding of the Word of God. We must begin to seek the Lord for the full understanding of his word:

> Study to show thyself approved unto God, a workman that needed not to be ashamed, rightly dividing the word of truth. (2 Timothy 2:15)

We are living in dark times in this world, and it's not a good idea to go around stumbling in the dark without the flashlight that is the Word of God. When we study the word of God, it is a lamp unto our feet, a light for our path. It tells us the obstacles to watch for and how to overcome them. It gives us clear directions if we take the time to study.

> All Scripture is given by inspiration of God, and is profitable for doctrine, for reproof, for correction, for instructions in righteousness. (2 Timothy 3:16)

All scripture is from God—it is all important, every jot and tittle. It's profitable for doctrine, our beliefs. It is good for reproof, to correct us when we're wrong, and it teaches us what is right. It doesn't get any better than this.

Jesus made sure he imparted the Spirit of Understanding to his disciples.

> Then said Jesus to them again, Peace be unto you: as my Father had sent me, even so send I you: And when he had said this, he breathed on them, and said unto them, Receive you the Holy Spirit. (John 20:21–22)

We know that Jesus operated without measure of the Spirit. We see him doing two things at one time: he spoke the peace upon them, and at the same time he blew upon them and they were instantly transformed. (This occasion came before the day of Pentecost.)

> Then opened he their understanding that they might understand the scriptures. (Luke 24:45)

Prosperity and Success

The Spirit of Understanding will make you prosperous and have good success in everything you are tasked with.

> This book of the law shall not depart out of thy mouth; but thou shall meditate therein day and night, that thou mayest observe to do according to all that is written therein: for then thou shall make thy way prosperous, and then thy shall have good success. (Joshua 1:8)

Understanding is a street we will always need to travel.

In All Your Getting, Get Understanding!

Solomon said, "Wisdom is the principal thing; therefore get wisdom: and with all thy getting get understanding" (Proverbs 4:7). Let's look at a parable to see why understanding is so important.

> Hearken; Behold, there went out sower to sow; And it came to pass, as he sowed, some fell by the way side, and the fowls of he air came and devoured it up … The sower soweth the word, And these are they by the way side, where the word is sown; but when they have heard it Satan cometh immediately and taketh away the word that was sown in their hearts. (Mark 4:3–4, 14–15)

Jesus was explaining that the word that was not understood was immediately stolen by the enemy. Therefore, it is imperative that we allow the Spirit of Understanding to assist us with the Word of God so that none of God's words are stolen by the enemy. And yes, if you know that Satan is a thief, then know now that he steals the words of God too.

I would like for you to pause in your reading, and ask for the Holy Spirit to give you complete understanding of God's Word and receive it as so.

CHAPTER 4

Street Name – The Spirit of Counsel

And the spirit of the Lord shall rest upon him,
the spirit of wisdom and understanding, the
spirit of counsel.

Isaiah 11:2

The Spirit of Counsel is the fourth manifestation of the Holy Spirit. His mode of operation is to guide you. He is the perfect street to walk on.

The psalmist David blesses the Lord, who has given him counsel and notes that "my reins also instruct me in the night season" (Psalm 16:7). When was the last time you blessed the Lord for giving you counsel? Better yet, when was the last time you asked God to instruct you in the night season?

Before reflecting on these questions, let's look at counsel from the perspective of Acts, chapter 16.

> Now when they [Paul, Silas, and Timothy]
> had gone throughout Phrygia and the
> region of Galatia, … [they] were forbidden
> of the Holy Spirit to preach the word in
> Asia. (Acts 16:6)

But verses 7–9 go on to report that

> after they were come to Mysia, they assayed
> to go into Bithynia: but the Spirit suffered
> them not, And they passing by Mysia came
> down to Troas.

The Spirit persuaded them not to take the route they had planned. Sometimes the Holy Spirit may not let you preach the good news in certain regions when he has not given you the "unction to function." He may have a different route for you to walk.

Always ask the Spirit of Counsel before you go to any region of the world to spread the gospel. I know this may shock some, because we have been told to go into all the world and preach the gospel—the good news. This is true, but it is still down to the Spirit of Counsel *where* you ought to preach the good news.

In Acts 11:11–12, the Spirit counseled Peter while he was praying in Simon's house:

> And behold immediately there were three
> men already come unto the house where I
> was, sent from Caesarea unto me. And the
> Spirit bade me go with me.

The Spirit of Counsel instructed Peter to go with these men and preach the gospel to them in Caesarea.

Finding the Right Direction

Do you feel that you are headed in the wrong direction in this season of your life? The good news is that the Spirit of Counsel can redirect your path.

> You will hear a voice behind you say, "No this is the way; walk here." (Isaiah 30:21)

If you answered my opening question with, "Yes, my life is headed in the wrong direction," how comforting it is to know that you can ask the Spirit of Counsel to redirect your path now.

> And his name shall be called Wonderful, Counsellor, The mighty God, The everlasting Father the Prince of Peace. (Isaiah 9:6)

So be it unto you according to the word of the Lord.

The Spirit of Counsel is an extraordinary strategist. He goes beyond the ordinary mind or senses. He operates in the supernatural, not the natural. There is no confusion in him. He knows how to get you out of every bad decision you will ever make, every crisis you will ever encounter, every dark place you may end up in. He knows how to make you a success.

Even before the pandemic, I had a few companies I had

to shut down because of the economy and where I was in my life. It was not an easy decision—to be downright honest, it was very hard. I had so much pressure on me. We have all heard the expression, "I didn't know if I was coming or going," and to that I can attest.

The Spirit of Counsel directed my attorney on how to work my case. At first when he told me how we would go about it, I really didn't like it; my flesh crawled. I began asking him all kinds of questions with all these papers in front of me. It was overwhelming just looking at the debt. Finally, I said to him, "I paid you for the job, and I will follow your lead."

The process was very arduous and downright unpleasant, but the Lord carried me through the entire process for two years. And because my attorney heard from the Spirit of Counsel, I was released of all debts and able to start fresh. I have not looked back since.

Trust the process when the Spirit of Counsel is working, and you will always come out on top!

There Is Victory in Your Steps

God raised Queen Esther to a position in the royal palace for a holy purpose. We speak often about how God prepared her for the king but not as often about the assignment she was to fulfill for the Jewish people.

Esther was an extraordinary strategist in the face of war, saying "If I perish, I perish" (Esther 4:16). Her courageous act would require her to put her own life in danger, but she was prepared before she entered the palace. God will always prepare you for the assignment ahead of you.

The assignment was pivotal: Esther dared to approach King Xerxes on behalf of her people, knowing that the death penalty awaited anyone who entered his presence uninvited. I believe that the Spirit of Counsel was leading Esther the whole way and instructing her what to do. We can see throughout the scriptures that he silently moves and directs her path: how she instructed everyone to fast for three days in mourning and prayer; how she begged for mercy from the king and was granted favor to complete the assignment.

If you don't know the complete story, I would encourage you to read the entire book of Esther to see how marvelously the Spirit of Counsel guided her and the Jewish people to victory!

I would like you to pause for a moment and think about a time when the Spirit of Counsel was guiding you—and you may not even have known it until you were out of danger or had achieved the victory.

The Great Strategist

In the biblical story of Joseph, often what people home in on is what his brothers did to him. But let's shed a different light on this story and look how the Spirit of Counsel was leading Joseph and instructing him.

Here again the Spirit of Counsel was silently leading him the whole way so that Joseph would be able to go and prepare for his family to be saved in the years to come. He walked it out. It was not an easy journey; Joseph had to encounter many difficult trials, as we all do, but he kept his faith in God and came out victorious. He was restored, revived, and renewed despite a terrible famine.

Joseph collected all the money that was to be found in Egypt and Canaan in payment for the grain they were buying, and he brought it to Pharaoh's palace.

> There was no food, however, in the whole region because the famine was severe; both in Egypt and Canaan wasted away because of the famine. (Genesis 47:13–17)

When the money of the people of Egypt and Canaan was gone, all Egypt came to Joseph and said, "Give us food. Why should we die before your eyes? Our money is all gone."

"Then bring your livestock," said Joseph. "I will sell you food in exchange for your livestock, since your money is gone."

So they brought their livestock to Joseph, and he gave them food in exchange for their horses, their sheep and goats, their cattle and donkeys. And he brought them through that year with food in exchange for all their livestock. I believe the Great Strategist the Holy Spirit was on board, making everything happen as it should have.

Here let us pause and thank the Spirit of Counsel for being the strategist of our lives and giving us the strategies we will need in the coming days to sustain our families, friends, and communities.

I thank God for the opportunity to have attended the 2022 Joseph Summit held in Orlando, Florida, under the administration of Prophet Joshua Giles. What I received there has inspired much of this chapter of my book. May God continue to bless him for his obedience to his word.

CHAPTER 5

Street Name – The Spirit of Might

And there shall come forth a rod out of the stem of Jesse, and a Branch shall grow out of his roots: And the spirit of the Lord shall rest upon him, the spirit of wisdom and understanding, The spirit of counsel and might.

Isaiah 11:1–2

The Spirit of Might, or mightiness, is the fifth of the Seven Spirits of God listed in Isaiah 11:2. There was a man by the name of Samson who operated in the Spirit of Might. He didn't walk with the wisdom of God—we know that by what took place in his life—but he operated in the Spirit of Might.

> Then went Samson down, and his father and his mother to Timnath, and came to the vineyards of Timnath; and behold a

> young lion roared against him. And the
> Spirit of the Lord came mightily upon him,
> and he rent him as he would have rent a kid,
> and he had nothing in his hand: but he told
> not his father or his mother what he had
> done. (Judges 14:5–6)

The Bible specifies a young lion, not a weak old lion whose days were coming to an end. The lion was full of strength and in the prime of his life.

When Samson saw the lion, he didn't ask for human help, nor did he ask which way to run, but in an instant the Spirit of the Lord came mightily upon him and he tore the lion apart with nothing but his hands. That is the Spirit of Might operating. Samson knew where his help came from, so there was no need to brag or go telling anyone.

> And when he came unto Lehi, the
> Philistines shouted against him; and the
> Spirit of the Lord came mightily upon
> him and cords that were upon his arms
> became as flax that was burnt with fire,
> and his bands loosed from off his hands.
> And he found a new jawbone of an ass and
> put forth his hand and took it and slew a
> thousand men therewith. (Judges 15:14–15)

When the Spirit of Might would come upon Samson, he became a changed man. He could not do any of this in his own strength, but he was a force to be reckoned with because the Lord was with him and the Might of God came upon him to do the seemingly impossible. The Might of God took over what we call the sensory mechanism.

This Might was even more in evidence after the Philistines had captured Samson and gouged out his eyes. They bought him out to entertain them during a feast in the temple of Dagon. Then Samson prayed, "O Lord God remember me, I pray thee, and strengthen me, I pray thee only this once, O God, that I may be at once to avenged of the Philistines for my two eyes" (Judges 16:28). After he prayed, the Spirit of Might came upon him and gave him supernatural strength such as he had in the past.

As I'm writing, something of the pain and anguish that Samson must have felt sweeps over me. He could not see; he must have been in a lot of emotional pain; he probably felt bad because he hadn't obeyed God fully and as a result found himself in this horrible situation, even to the point of blindness and death. But God in his mercy allowed the Spirit of Might to come upon him once more as he prayed, and he defeated his enemies and in the end killed more Philistines in death than in his lifetime.

Samson went out with a bang! Only the Spirit of Might can do that.

I'm reminded of when David, being full of the Spirit, charged after a lion, delivered a lamb from its mouth, and killed the lion. He shouted, "I caught it by its beard!" I know David must have known about Samson and his acts and been impressed by them, because David continued as a mighty warrior of God. The Spirit of Might came upon him when he faced Goliath of Gath, the Philistine giant. David told Goliath how he would end up like those beasts he had already devoured, and that is exactly what happened. All this happened when the Spirit of Might was in operation.

The Spirit of Might causes you to be bold, endowed with strength from on high, and overcoming every situation. Isaiah prophesied concerning the Lord Jesus and called him the Might of God, the one who is clothed in strength and has overpowered everything this life has to offer (Isaiah 9:6).

To conclude this chapter, let's take a moment to ask the Holy Spirit of Might to begin today to operate in our lives and in the lives of our families and communities—to help us achieve and do the impossible for his kingdom.

CHAPTER 6

Street Name –
The Spirit of Knowledge

And the spirit of the Lord shall rest upon him ... the spirit of knowledge.

Isaiah 11:2

Your limitations in relation to what you have achieved thus far is a direct result of whether the Spirit of Knowledge has been leading you and guiding you through the affairs of your life. You may not have known that the Spirit of Knowledge is one of the manifestations of the Holy Spirit. If you knew, continue to seek his knowledge. If you did not know, ask him today to help you so that you can live your best life on this earth. If you knew that the Spirit of Knowledge could work in your life, why wouldn't you ask for it?

Revealed Knowledge

Revealed knowledge means exactly that: knowledge that has been revealed rather than acquired through human reason and study efforts. The Holy Spirit specializes in the absolute knowledge of God. This knowledge is beyond compare to our finite minds. It transcends the mental realm or anything having to do with normality.

When the Spirit of Knowledge reveals what God's purpose and will is to you, there is not a shadow of a doubt: he makes it plain in a way that even a child would understand. You receive this knowledge only by listening, not by reasoning. For many Christians, this has been a pain point: they want to reason with the Holy Spirit and not just accept that his word is the absolute truth—there is no plan B because he is exact in everything he does. If there is a plan B, it's on your end, not his.

The Holy Spirit cannot make a mistake and does not have the ability to lie. So even as you are reading the words on this page today, you can free yourself of doubt and go with the Spirit of Knowledge that he is imparting in you. It would behoove you to just do it. Don't think with your head; listen to your heart. When you listen to your heart, it is revelation from the Spirit of Knowledge.

When you know something by the Spirit of Knowledge, you walk boldly in it. When you know something by your own knowledge, you will walk in doubt no matter how you try to convince yourself it's right. You will not have God's kind of peace.

Revelation is a force that imparts knowledge, works in your mind, renews your thought to truly live, and causes you to have the advantage in life. The Spirit of Knowledge will bring awareness where needed.

> Now we have received, not the spirit of the world, but the spirit which is of God; that we might know the things that are freely given to us of God. (1 Corinthians 2:12)

I believe God is saying to become aware of what you have been given and begin to take advantage of these things and not just take it lightly. You have a force that is in you and wants to guide you and help you figure out anything that you will need in this life. There is no reason to feel hopeless. You have been given too much even to begin to think in this way.

Let's pause here so that you can ask the Spirit of Knowledge to guide you through your life's affairs with peace.

Be Full of Understanding!

In Ephesians 3:17–19, Paul gets to his knees and prays

> that Christ may dwell in your hearts by faith; that ye, being rooted and grounded in love, May be able to comprehend with all the saints what is the breadth, and length, and depth, and height; And to know the love of Christ, which passes knowledge, that ye might be filled with all the fullness of God.

What Paul is saying is to know the love of Christ by revelation, and the only way we can know this is through the Spirit of Knowledge.

If you are not rooted or grounded in love, please take a moment now and ask the Holy Spirit of Knowledge to help you in this area. His love passes what we think we know about love. This love is not fleshly; it goes beyond comprehension, as I am reminded by John 3:16: *"for God so loved the world that he gave his only begotten Son."* Do you love something you would give up for someone else even though you love it so much? Probably not, truth be told. But God is not asking you to give anything up to prove your love. He is just asking you to be rooted and grounded in love, and this I believe you can handle.

CHAPTER 7

Street Name —
The Fear of the Lord

And the spirit of the Lord shall rest upon him,
the spirit of wisdom and understanding, the
spirit of counsel and might, the spirit of
knowledge and of the fear of the Lord.

Isaiah 11:2

The fear of the Lord is the last but certainly not the least of the Seven Spirits of God that Isaiah 11:2 lists.

> The fear of the Lord is the beginning of knowledge; fools despise wisdom and instructions. (Proverbs 1:7)

What this scripture is telling me is that when we have a reverential fear of the Lord, he provides knowledge to navigate our paths in this life. There is no reason to look to the world because the answers are not there. People bound to the world are searching themselves without the Holy Spirit of Knowledge, and there are no true answers outside of him.

During the pandemic, I believe that everyone was searching to find knowledge, because his children feared the Lord in a holy way. I can attest that the Holy Spirit gave us knowledge to get through the tough times and come out on top. No lives were lost in my family or those I am connected to. Psalms 91 and 121, two of my mother's favorite passages of scripture and mine as well, talk about no plague coming nigh to our dwelling, as well as the Lord preserving our going in and coming out. Lord knows we needed that during the pandemic, and still do! We didn't know whom we would meet or what would be borne in the air in the places we visited.

I beckon you to set aside time to read both these psalms in full, soon after reading this book or tomorrow. They will bless your life even if you have read them a thousand times. I believe you will find new meaning and see something you have never seen before. The Word of God is alive and always breathing life into us.

Praise God! He infuses his faithful ones with wisdom, guidance, instructions, and whatever we may need at the appointed time. He goes before us to make the crooked places straight. Isn't that good news? You never have to worry about stumbling if you acknowledge him. Remember, the fear of the Lord is the beginning of knowledge.

As you rise each day, thank the Holy Spirit for knowledge in your daily task. Never take him for granted, though he is always there to assist you. Just ask him, and he will make every path straight.

Let's take a moment to meditate on the fear of the Lord.

He has made his wonderful works to be remembered. The Lord is gracious and full of compassion. He has given food to those who fear him; he will ever be mindful of His covenant. He has declared to his people the power of his works in giving them the heritage of the nations. The works of his hands are verity and justice; all his precepts are sure. They stand fast forever and ever and are done in truth and uprightness. He has sent redemption to his people; he has commanded His covenant forever. Holy and awesome is His name. The fear of the Lord is the beginning of wisdom; a good understanding have all those who do His commandments. His praise endures forever.

Fire from Heaven

I am reminded of Elijah calling down fire from heaven and how the people greatly feared the Lord.

> So Elijah answered and said to them If I be a man of God, Let fire come down from heaven and consume you and your fifty men. And the fire of God came down from heaven and consumed him and his fifty. (2 Kings 1:12)

Elijah was confident in the God of Israel, and he feared the Lord greatly seen in his life. Even during his greatest victories and trials, the battle was always won because he feared the Lord. I named my son Elijah so that he would always remember the fear of the Lord will give you victory in life every time!

Samuel was one of the greatest prophets and priests who ever lived on the face of the earth. He called on the Lord to send thunder and rain, and all the people greatly feared the Lord (1 Samuel 12:18). We know that the Spirit of the Lord's hand was all in this. The Bible also says that the people feared Samuel as well. That tells me that when you fear God, people will see his works and fear you as well, and therefore when you are doing the will of the Father, there is no need to fear people. Go ahead and call down fire, thunder, and rain! And watch your God move in miraculous ways.

We must get back to having a reverential fear of the Lord. I insist that we reverence God in our prayer time, giving, ministry, homes, and workplace. Let's not walk in our own flesh and do things deceitfully, as Ananias and Sapphira misbehaved, losing all respect for the fear of the Lord. We know that when they did, they were struck dead immediately, and the fear of the Lord came upon the people (Acts 5:1–11).

I truly believe we are in those times again, where some have lost reverence for the Most High God. We have seen over the years how these actions have increased. Many have fallen dead on the spot without warning, and fear came upon the people. Sometimes it seems as though people see this happening and turn their faces so as not to face reality. But I believe during the days we are living in there won't be a face able to turn or a way of escape. God will show his power, and men will begin to repent and turn back to God with the fear of the Lord in their hearts once again.

Let's not live in fear but get excited about the end times. There is no stopping it even if you wanted to!

Humility and Purity

Humility is key. The fear of the Lord will cause you to be a humble person. You will not be a person puffed up in pride. You will always live in a lowly place because you revere and fear God. You will not be a person who will judge unrighteously or be quick to point the finger, knowing that we all have sinned and fallen short of the glory of God. You will live with an open heart to love and assist those in need; the Bible says when we do this, we lend to God. Why not become a lender to God and not man? The interest that comes back is more than compounded.

Religion that God our Father accepts as pure and faultless involves looking after orphans and widows in their distress and keeping oneself from being polluted by the world (James 1:27). This is one of my truest passions: taking care of orphans and widows. No one has the ability to take care of everyone in the world, but everyone has a part to play. Whatever God has commissioned your hands to do, just do it and don't waste any more time so that our Father in heaven may be glorified.

Stop running after false gods. Live in the eye-opening season when the blinders are taken off the eyes of God's people and they are no longer blind, nor do they sleep anymore. It's the time of the awakening.

God is putting his people's hearts back in position to do his perfect will and not to be so materialistic that you lose sight of the Great Commission. I'm not against having things; the Word of God says, "Seek you first the kingdom of God and all these things will be added unto you" (Matthew

6:33). I have been very blessed and continue to be in life, but my true passion is helping God's people.

When you say "blessed," most people's minds go right to money. It doesn't have to be monetary; blessings can come in other forms if you are an underwriter for the kingdom of God! Let's all be underwriters, for there are a lot of souls that need to be saved and shown the glory of the Father.

> Then the king will say to those on His right hand, Come, you blessed of My father, inherit the kingdom prepared for you from the foundation of the world. For I was hungry, and you gave Me food; I was thirsty, and you gave me drink; I was a stranger, and you took Me in. I was naked an you clothed Me; I was sick and you visited Me; I was in prison and you came to Me. (Matthew 25:34–36)

I believe this scripture sums it up!

Let's take a moment and meditate on living in humility and allowing God to exalt us in due season. Let's not live in haste and want.

I'd like to close by echoing the words of Paul the apostle in asking you to submit yourselves to one another in the fear of God (1 Peter 5:5). Let's all be subject to one another in love and clothed in humility. Revere and allow him to admonish you, and he will exalt you in due season.

CLOSING WORDS

Now that you have read about the Seven Spirits and the fullness of God and the ways the Holy Spirit can give you the advantage in life, my prayer is that you get to know him in a deeper and fulfilling way in the coming days. You are going to need it to be able to navigate through life's mountains and valleys, and to be there for anyone whom God has assigned to you.

Let the Holy Spirit work in your life so that you begin to live a life that is balanced and stress-free. You can stop participating in the "I don't know what to do" way of thinking. You will be able to say, "I know exactly what to do." Remember, the Spirit of God is the most knowledgeable life coach you will ever need to guide and give you the best advice that no man on this earth can come close to.

May the peace of God fill your hearts and minds. As you go forth and do great exploits, always remember that the seven manifestations of the Holy Spirit are at your disposal 100 percent of the time. Just ask for what you need.

Shalom!

Printed in the United States
by Baker & Taylor Publisher Services

MONEY HUNGRY

Sharon G. Flake

JUMP AT THE SUN

HYPERION PAPERBACKS FOR CHILDREN

NEW YORK

This paperback edition was reissued by Jump at the Sun in 2007.
7 9 10 8

Printed in United States of America

Library of Congress Cataloging-in-Publication Data on file.
ISBN-13: 978-1-4231-0386-8
ISBN-10: 1-4231-0386-6
Visit www.jumpatthesun.com
V 4 7 5 - 2 8 7 3 - 0 - 1 3 1 5 8

To Judy Suh and Richard, who stood in the gap,

to Robin, Carla, and Sandra,
my writing buddies; my friends

to my Harold Street Neighbors,
who are always in my heart

and to the students, teachers, and librarians
around the country who have embraced my work
and treated me with such warmth and kindness

thank you, thank you, thank you!

CHAPTER ONE

Some people think I would do anything for money. They're wrong. I wouldn't do nothing bad. Nothing that would hurt people, like selling dope, or shoplifting. But when you always trying to think of ways to make a dollar, like I do, folks bound to think the worst.

Weird, huh? A thirteen-year-old girl who loves money. Who got bunches of it—nickels, quarters, dollars—stashed under her bed, shoved in socks, piled in drawers.

Some nights, when I can't sleep, I grab me a fistful and count it till I drop off snoring. Don't take me too long to nod off then. No wonder everybody thinks that my money-hungry ways will get me into more trouble than I can handle. Shoot, even my girls think that. My momma, too.

Momma. She and me is usually tight. But this morning, I ain't even speaking to her. Yesterday, I seen her getting out of that Lexus, kissing Dr. Mitchell, my girlfriend's divorced dad, on the cheek. Laughing, like he was soooo funny.

I don't ever remember Momma dating nobody. Not since she and Daddy got divorced a few years back. It ain't so bad she's dating somebody, but she could at least be straight up with me about it, especially since it's Zora's dad she's hanging with.

"Time for school, Raspberry," she says, marching from room to room, slamming drawers shut, and turning off our dripping faucets.

I'm in the bathroom rubbing pimple cream on my face. Hoping it will make this zit family sitting right on my chin go away before school starts this morning.

When I get to the kitchen, bacon's popping around in the pan. It's Valentine's Day, and

Momma's got heart-shaped cinnamon pan-
cakes lying on a pretty red-and-white plate on
the table.

I tell Momma to hurry up. I got to make me
some money today. She shakes her head. All
this money talk gets on her nerves, she always
saying. But I don't care. I'm gonna have me
some big-time cash someday. I ain't gonna be
stuck up here in the projects, trying to get by
like everybody else.

Momma turns her head my way, and
smiles. "Sit," she says, patting the kitchen
chair.

I grab a paper towel to rub that zit cream
off my face before it dries. Don't want it chip-
ping off like plaster from a wall and falling in
my food like it did last time.

"Eat," Momma says, putting five pieces of
bacon on my plate and setting down a bowl of
warm syrup. She's on another diet, so all she's
eating is dry toast.

Momma don't even realize I ain't speaking
to her. She's going on and on about the table.
How pretty it looks. It's got a white plastic
tablecloth on it, with pink candy hearts—

sprinkled from end to end. There's also a homemade card sitting there waiting for me to read.

I had a Valentine's card for Momma, too, until last night, when I seen her with Dr. Mitchell. After that, I ripped that thing into a thousand tiny pieces. Tossed it out my bedroom window, even though Momma's the head of the tenant cleanup committee, and she don't play stuff like that.

CHAPTER TWO

Momma's putting on her coat, saying she's gonna go heat up the car so we don't freeze our butts off on the way to school. I put the last of the bacon in my mouth, and go check myself out in the mirror to make sure there ain't no gunk stuck between my teeth. Then I'm out the door, coat and all. Soon as I step into the hallway of our building, I hold my nose with my fingers. I can tell that Shoe and his brother Check been peeing up the place again. In the summer, they say they do it to kill off the ants. Wintertime they claim they killing roaches and spiders. I think they just trying to see who can pee the farthest. I don't know why they even bother.

Before the weekend comes, Momma gonna have 'em down here scrubbing up. Then their grandma's gonna go upside their heads for being so nasty in the first place. It happens like this all the time.

I'm trying hard not to breathe in this funky stuff. But it's hard holding your breath and locking up fast when you got three locks to work with.

By the time I get to the street, Momma's giving Shoe an earful, yelling out the car window at him for doing something he shouldn't. That boy got a lot of nerve for an eleven-year-old. He's standing on the curb next to the car, loud-talking Momma. Saying he didn't pee in the hallway. But everybody round here knows peeing in the hallways is Shoe and Check's trademark, kinda like Zorro with his Z, or Spiderman with his web.

I'm on the sidewalk sitting in a busted-up chair, watching Momma and Shoe go at each other. Momma tells Shoe he better not make her get out her car and get next to him. He's got his eyes fixed on her good. Then he does what he shoulda done in the first place. He backs down, and mumbles some lame apology. That's when Momma gives the car a little gas, and pulls out of her parking space.

I get up out the chair, and sit it in Momma's empty parking space so nobody takes it while she's gone. Momma don't see, but Shoe kicks over the chair soon as our car pulls off.

Usually, when Momma drives me to school, I'm talking her ears off. Since she works nights, we use our mornings to catch up on things. But today, I ignore her. I turn the radio on, and start jammin' to the beat. I act like Momma ain't even here.

By the time we get to the bottom of the hill, Momma says, "We need to talk." Good, I'm thinking. She gonna tell me what's up with her and Zora's dad. But no, Momma turns down the radio and starts talking about hormones, and how thirteen-year-old girls like me get moody because we're turning into women.

I want to let her know that my hormones is fine. That it's *her* that's making me act this way. But before I can say anything, she's rolling down the window, minding somebody else's business.

"Maleek Johnson," Momma shouts. "If you don't get off that girl, I'll tell your mother soon as I get home."

Maleek stops kissing Sissy. Then he tells his boys to shut up when they start laughing at him. Me, I slump down in the seat of the car. Way down, hoping no one sees me.

"Dag, Momma," I say. "Why you have to go and do that?"

Our car is stopped at the light at Jackson and Thorp. Kids waiting to cross the street stare right in my face, like it was me busting up Maleek's good time.

Maleek's face is all red now. Only he ain't the only one embarrassed. I am, too. Bad enough we ride around in the oldest car on the planet. Why do Momma have to make it worse by always drawing attention to us? Always minding other folks' business.

When Momma finishes with Maleek, she rolls up the car window, and steps on the gas. I turn the radio up and close my eyes. I'm gonna make me some big-time cash today, so I concentrate on that, not Momma.

After six blocks of me not saying nothing, Momma asks me, "What's wrong?"

I don't want to say nothing. But the words come out before I can stop 'em. I look dead in her eyes and ask, "What's up with you and Zora's dad?"

Momma's body jerks back a little, like you do when somebody steps out from behind a door when you ain't expecting it. Then she tries to act like she's cool. "Don't look at me like that," she says, making sure her eyes don't meet mine.

For a long while, she don't even look where she's driving. She's messing around with the rearview mirror. Dusting crumbs off the seat. Stuff like that.

After a while, Momma tries to answer my question about her and Zora's dad. "Dr. Mitchell and I can do as we please. We grown. We *are* grown," she says, correcting her English. It makes me so mad, her doing that all day long. But since she started college last year, she's been trying to improve the way she speaks. I tell Momma to just leave me be.

I like how I talk just fine.

"Dr. Mitchell and me are friends, Raspberry. That's all," she says, putting on the brakes soon as we get to school.

I get the hint. Momma don't want to talk. I know something's up with them two. I put my hand out for lunch money, and jump out Momma's side of the car soon as she gives me the cash. I try not to do what I always do when dollars grease my palm—smell the money like it's chocolate-chip cookies straight out the oven.

Before I walk away, I turn around and say something I know is gonna hurt Momma bad. "He a *doctor*, Momma. What you think somebody like *him* wants with somebody like *you*, who lives in the projects with gangbangers and junkies?"

CHAPTER THREE

It's still early. First-period class ain't even started yet. Kids is hanging out in front of school.

"Raspberry Hill! You better get in here and straighten this mess up, girl!" Zora says, standing at the front door, with her arms folded tight.

I don't even say bye to Momma. I run Zora's way. She's selling a few things for me today, so if something's wrong, that means I ain't gonna get my money. And I ain't having that.

Zora's eyes is pumpkin-seed green today. Last week, they was the color of honey. Three weeks back, they was gray, blue, and black, all in one week. That's what happens when your parents is rolling in dough and can hook you up with contact lenses. But all that cash don't mean Zora got a dime to her name, especially since her parents' divorce. Since then, her life has changed big-time. Her dad pulled her out of a private school and put her in this-here magnet school. He cut off her allowance—$150 a month—and moved her back into the city with him. Now Zora's broke half the time. That's why she's trying to make a little dough with me today. She's hoping she can earn enough money to get those new sneakers she wants. They cost $120, and her dad says she's gotta pay half the cost if she wants 'em.

When I get inside, Seneca Mason pushes past Zora and shoves half a chocolate candy heart my way. "Zora selling these for you?" Seneca asks. Sato and Ja'nae are standing there not saying nothing. They just checking us out.

"Yeah," I say.

"So?" Zora says, giving her some attitude, like she can fight if things get tight.

"I should've known," Seneca says, getting loud.

"What you want, Seneca?" I say to her.

Seneca waves the candy bar in the air, making her voice get louder with every word she says. "I don't want this mess. Give me my money back."

"No refunds," Zora says, loud and slow, like she's talking to someone who don't understand English. "You ate half the candy. Now what do you want us to do?"

Seneca looks at Zora. Then she takes her fat, crooked middle finger and shoves it deep inside her mouth. She drags her finger across her gums, around her teeth. Then out comes her finger, covered with mashed-up chocolate chunks and shiny spit bubbles.

"Dag. That look like it came out your butt," Sato says, frowning up his face at Ja'nae.

"Shut up, Sato," Zora, me, and Seneca all say together.

"Here's the rest," Seneca says, holding up her finger. "You want it?"

Zora and me back off. Seneca reaches in

her pocketbook and grabs a balled-up piece of paper and wipes off her finger.

She puts her hand on her hip, then sticks her other hand way out like she got a million dollars coming her way. "Now give me my money."

"No-class girls like you are the reason my mother wants me to transfer out of this school," Zora says, rubbing her white cashmere sweater.

"Good. When you leaving, zipper mouth?" Seneca says, talking about Zora's braces.

Zora acts like she didn't hear Seneca crack on her. But I saw her cheek jump when Seneca's words came out. Before Seneca says anything else, I shove my hand in my pocket and give her fifty cents of the lunch money Momma gave me in the car.

"You better be ready to give *all* that money back," Seneca says, "'cause nobody's gonna eat that mess you're selling."

Seneca's right. Before homeroom period is up, eight more people want their money back. The last four kids are out of luck, though.

I ain't walking out of school today with nothing. I mean, I gotta show *something* for all me and Zora's hard work. But a few minutes later here comes Zenna Greene walking up to me. "I don't feel so good," she says, rubbing her stomach. "That candy is making me sick."

I got my hand in my pocket. I'm feeling the money I made, that Zora made for me. I gotta give Zora fifteen percent. That was our deal. But that's gonna be fifteen percent of nothing if I keep giving money back to kids who bought the candy and hated it. I wrap my fingers around the money that's in my pocket. "Maybe your stomach hurts 'cause you ate something else," I say, starting to walk away from Zenna.

"Give me my money back," Zenna says, grabbing me back with her loud, squeaky voice.

Zenna is holding her side. Rubbing her stomach. Zenna Greene, Miss Drama Queen, trying to get some attention, I say to myself.

"I gotta go to the bathroom," she says, trying to make a run for it.

But it's too late. Stuff starts flying out her mouth. Slimy, chocolate-colored stuff. Spaghetti pieces. Chewed-up meat. It all comes splashing over the hard, shiny waxed floor. Kids is screaming and laughing and running out the way.

"You got my new shoes, girl!" somebody says.

"Man, it stinks," Ja'nae says, holding her nose.

Zenna's still holding her stomach when the principal, Mr. Jackson, walks over. He tells Zenna to go to the nurse. Yells for a teacher to call the janitor.

"Must be a bug," Mr. Jackson says, shaking his head.

"Ain't no bug. It's Raspberry. She's hustling chocolate that got worms in it," Seneca says, butting in my business.

Mr. Jackson don't even ask me if that lie is true or not. He sticks out his gigantic hand and says, "Fork it over."

I hand him one of the chocolate hearts. He unwraps it real slow, like it's a bomb or something. "You trying to kill somebody?" he says, eyeballing the candy, then throwing it into the trash.

"Raspberry don't care if she kill nobody, long as they pay up before they die," Sato says, laughing.

I look down in the trash at the candy. It got big, dry, white patches on it like the crust you see on a scab that's ready to fall off. But the candy ain't *that* stale. I got them for two cents apiece last year after Valentine's Day was over. The salesman said I could freeze 'em to keep 'em fresh. So I kept 'em in Ja'nae's basement freezer since then.

The principal closes in on me. "Your mother know you're selling this mess?"

"Yeah! No, I mean," I say, fumbling with my words. "She knows I was gonna sell something. But she don't know what it was, really."

"Well, let's give her a little call," Mr. Jackson says, grabbing me by the elbow and dragging me down the hall. Mr. Jackson is saying something else about calling Momma. Me, I'm holding tight to my ducats. 'Cause no matter what, I'm not giving up no more cash today.

CHAPTER FOUR

I knew it. Zenna didn't get sick off my candy. She's got the flu. The nurse said she was even running a fever. But not too many people here talking about *that*. They're still running off at the mouth about me, saying how I was selling poison candy in school yesterday.

Mr. Jackson told me not to sell no more candy. But he didn't say nothing about selling other stuff. So today, I'm at it again. Selling red valentine pencils with purple heart-shaped erasers on top. They're discounted though, since Valentine's Day is done and gone.

"Thirty cents," I say to Eric Kelly when we're in the lunchroom. But he's not hardly paying me any attention. He's eyeing Zora, with her smooth, cocoa-brown skin, and that dimple in her left cheek. Eric can't even eat his cheeseburger, he's staring at her so much.

"You want it or not?" I say, putting my hand out for the money.

"What you do with all the money you make off us?" he says, wiping cheeseburger juice off his chin with the back of his hand.

"Yeah," Charles Taylor says, finishing off his lunch—a giant-size Snickers bar and a Big Gulp Pepsi. "You always got some scam going. Gotta be making money off somebody or you ain't happy."

I don't say nothing to Eric or Charles. I just take out my pencils and start counting how many I still got to sell. I'm doing the math in my head. Hmmm. I sold ten pencils in math class. I still got twenty left.

"You want one or not, Eric?" I ask. "Zora likes purple, you know. It's her favorite color. Right, Zora?" I say, poking her in the side.

She ain't paying neither one of us any attention. She's staring at herself in a mirror she got in her hand. Me, I don't look in mirrors too often. I don't need no reminders of why my mother named me after a piece of fruit. I got red hair, red eyebrows, and enough freckles on my face that you can play connect the dots. Nope, that ain't the kind of face I wanna be looking at unless I absolutely have to.

"Zora, tell him," I say, reaching over and taking one of her carrot sticks.

She still watching herself in her mirror, like she expecting her eyes to change color or something. "Yeah, whatever Raspberry says, that's right," she says, drawing back her lips, so she can get a good look at her teeth. They got pink braces on 'em.

"Forget it," I say, walking away from both of them. Then I spend the next twenty minutes going from table to table trying to sell them things.

"You rich yet?" Sato asks me.

"She makes enough money off us to buy herself a house," Charles Gordon says.

"Nothing wrong with doing a little business," I say, stepping over Sato's raggedy book bag. "Maybe you could buy yourself a new book bag if you worked for me, Sato."

"Oh man, you gonna let her play you like that?" one of his boys says.

"Man. Forget her," Sato says, sticking out his foot like he's trying to trip me up. "My bag may be whacked, but at least I sleep in a bed at night. Not under no bridge like a troll."

Before I know anything, I'm throwing them pencils right at Sato's big blockhead. But that don't make him shut up.

"I guess the projects seem like the White House to you," Sato says, getting loud. "I mean, so what if you got holes in the walls and rats biting your feet at night."

"We don't have no—" I start defending myself, but Sato cuts me off.

"It's better than living out a cardboard box and washing up in the gas station bathroom like you used to, huh?"

Sato knows how to crack on people good. So I don't give him a chance to say nothing else. I pick up my pencils and go.

Momma and me never lived under no bridge. But when things got bad, real bad a few years back, we did live in a junkyard not far from here. We slept in a old beat-up van that was up on blocks. It didn't have no wheels. And the front window was busted. The mosquitoes ate us up good all summer long. One night, I counted fifteen bites.

We wasn't always broke. We was renting us a nice house, in a half-decent neighbor-hood, till Daddy started hanging out. Coming in with the sun, Momma used to say. I still don't know how it happened. One day he was Daddy. Going to work all day long, and hug-ging me good-night before I fell asleep at night. The next day it seemed like he was somebody else. Arguing about money all the time. Walking off with our TV, or Momma's old fur jacket. Dragging home friends that looked like they just got out of lockdown. Meeting me after school with his hand out . . . begging for whatever change I had.

When the dope made him so crazy he beat Momma up and sent her to the hospital for the third time, Momma left him. We lived with friends and family till they got tired of us. Then we lived in a motel till Momma got laid off work, and our money ran out. We went back to living with some of Momma's friends till they started hinting about how crowded their place was, and how much I eat. Next thing I knew, we was living outside with stray cats and dogs. Dirty men. Crazy women. Kids without parents, and people pushing shopping carts filled with smashed-up pop cans and wrinkled-up newspapers.

People said Momma should go to one of them shelters for women and kids. She wouldn't. She said she was in a shelter when she was little, and something bad happened to her there. Only she never would say what. So we slept on the street, and in dark corners of tall, empty buildings. We washed up in gas stations and fast-food restaurants. Asked for handouts. Prayed real hard that nobody would knock us in the head, or try to steal the little bit of stuff we had.

No matter how bad it got, though, I never missed a day of school in all the time we was living on the street. And I never missed saving Momma a little of the free lunch they gave me in school. Cold Tater Tots taste like steak when that's all you got.

Momma's the kind of person that don't let her surroundings mess with her head. So every night, when we lived in the van, she would sit in the driver's seat, look up at the stars, and tell me how things was gonna be. "One day," she'd say, "we gonna have our own place. With a family room, and a fireplace. What color room you want? Yeah, I figured you'd want blue . . . but what about letting me paint some clouds on the walls for you? And a few stars, so we don't forget that even bad times is sprinkled with a little good," she'd say, reaching up at the sky like she was gonna grab a fistful of stars and hand 'em to me.

After we got off the street, Momma had some job stuffing envelopes at night. Sometimes we would be down to just rice, beans, and Kool-Aid. You know what it's like to eat beans every night for two weeks straight? To drink Kool-Aid without sugar?

Even now, Momma's always dreaming about the future. But you can't cash dreams in at the bank or buy bread, or pay rent with 'em. You need hard, cold cash for that. So every penny I get, I save. Momma thinks I just got a little pocket change stashed here and there. But nickels don't keep you off the street. That's why I got six hundred dollars stashed all over my room.

You gotta sell a lot of pencils and skip a lot of lunches to make that kinda dough. But it's worth it. 'Cause if you got money, people can't take stuff from you—not your house, or your ride, not your family. They can't do nothing much to you, if you got a bankroll backing you up.

CHAPTER FIVE

Even though I'm not supposed to, I sold some more stuff at school today. So on my way to Zora's house, I'm using the calculator to figure out how much money I made. I'm so busy counting dollars that I don't notice I'm on the express bus. It doesn't stop for six blocks now.

Two old ladies run off at the mouth all the time I'm on this bus. They're complaining about their arthritis and grandkids who don't never come by or call. Stuff like that.

But then they say something that makes me listen up. One of 'em says that the hardest part about being old is not being able to keep her place clean like before.

"I can't hardly pick up my eyeglasses, let alone pick up a bucket and scrub down the place," she says.

Soon as one of 'em shuts up, the other one puts in her two cents' worth. "Girl, I ain't spending my golden years hauling trash and scrubbing floors, when I can be catching sales and eating out," she says, puffing up her hair. "I bring somebody else in to take care of that."

The short one, whose legs don't even touch the floor when she's sitting down, turns to her friend and says, "I paid a woman seventy-five dollars just to come and straighten up a little, and my house was still a mess after she left."

For a minute, they just sit there. Then one of 'em reaches up to grab hold of the cord overhead, and pulls it to let the driver know she wants off at the next stop.

"I don't use these triflin' cleaning women no more," she says, standing. "My neighbor's girl comes in and straightens up for me. She's fifteen, but she cleans as good as grown-ups do," she says, buttoning her coat, and standing to leave with her friend.

When they're gone, I clear my calculator

screen. There ain't nothing but some money waiting for me if I clean up some of them old people's places, I'm thinking.

While I'm walking the six blocks back to Zora's house, I'm smiling. Not even feeling the cold. Just thinking about getting paid seventy-five dollars just to clean somebody's place up. Shoot, Momma got me doing that at home for free.

By the time I'm around the corner from Zora's house, I got things figured out. If I can find some old people to clean up after, I can make a hundred fifty, two hundred dollars a week. My mouth starts watering just thinking about all that cash. I stop for a minute, and do some more figuring on my calculator. When I look up again, I see Zora's dad's car zoom by me. I guess he don't recognize me, all bundled up like I am.

Momma and me been knowing Zora and her dad since they moved around here three years ago. We saw 'em at the soup kitchen, while we was living in the streets. Dr. Mitchell brought Zora there because he wanted to show her how the other half lived. Said she was getting too snooty. Too sassy. Too much like her mother, I guess.

Me and Momma was at the soup kitchen serving stuff. When we wasn't doing that, we was way back in the corner, eating till our stomachs got full. Momma would never let us eat unless we cleaned and served others first.

Dr. Mitchell and Momma got to talking and it turned out they both come from the same place . . . the projects on the other side of town. Dr. Mitchell knew Momma's brother who got shot for four quarters and a bottle of beer on his twenty-first birthday.

When Dr. Mitchell found out we was living on the streets, he invited us to come stay at their place till we got back on our feet. Zora looked like she would die if we did that. Momma said no. She told Dr. Mitchell we would make out.

A couple months later, we finally got us a place in the projects. Our first night, Momma cried till the streetlights went off. She said she was just tired, but I think she was sad over ending up right back in the projects where she started out all them years ago.

CHAPTER SIX

Zora, Ja'nae, and Mai don't even say hi when I get upstairs. They tell me to shut up so they don't miss the show they're watching. I roll my eyes at them, and take me a slice of cold pizza sitting on the dresser.

We all live near each other. Mai's up here in Pecan Landings with Zora. I live five miles from here, up the tallest hill in the world. Folks say it's to keep us project kids from coming down to Pecan Landings and causing trouble. That don't stop me none. I'm down here all the time.

Ja'nae lives with her grandparents. She's younger than us three by five months. But you wouldn't know it. She's short and fat, and dresses like them old church women do, with skirts down past her knees. Her face is beautiful, though, especially her big, dark eyes. If you don't believe me, ask Mai's brother, Ming. He loves himself some Ja'nae. Ja'nae likes him, too. But Ja'nae knows ain't nothing gonna happen between her and Ming. Ja'nae's granddad is crazy. Ever since her mom took off, he keeps her in lockdown as much as he can. He thinks if he doesn't, Ja'nae will end up just like her mother.

"What took you so long?" Zora says to me when her show goes off.

I don't answer. I sit down on the floor next to her, and start talking about how we can make us some good money.

Soon as I open my mouth, Zora zips up the sleeping bag she's in till we can't see nothing but her ponytail. Mai puts on her earphones and turns it up so loud I can hear every word the band is singing. Ja'nae up and walks out the room. None of them want to hear me out.

I yell for 'em to listen up. Tell 'em I know how we can make us some decent dollars. Mai don't wanna hear it. "You always say that," she says. "It never do work out that way."

Ja'nae reaches in the pizza box and scrapes a clump of cheese off the box top. She rolls it into a small ball with the tip of her fingers, and flicks it into her mouth. "You too money hungry," she says.

"You just too hungry," I snap back.

Ja'nae's big eyes start to blink. She gets real quiet.

"Sorry," I say.

I been making my own money since I was four years old and my granddad paid me a quarter to clear his dinner plate when he came to visit. Later on, when Daddy was acting out and money got tight, I would go hunting for loose change on the street like a pigeon hunts for bread. On Saturdays I'd get up early and beg people to let me carry their groceries to their car. I'd pick their things up before they had a chance to say no. It helped, me being a girl. People would give me a dollar but still carry their own stuff. Much as I tried, I couldn't make enough money to keep Momma and me from ending up on the streets.

Now Zora and them are talking about how

greedy I am. How I'm always trying to make a dollar. They're right. But as long as I got two hands, I ain't never living in the street no more. Ain't never gonna be broke, neither.

When they're all quiet, I finally get to say what I gotta say. When I'm finished, they just stare at me. Then they bust out laughing. All three of 'em.

"You out your mind? I ain't cleaning nobody's house," Ja'nae says, frowning. She walks over to Zora's dresser, picks up a pair of gold hoop earrings, and asks if she can put them on.

"Sato's right," Zora says, shaking her head no to Ja'nae. "You'll do anything for a dollar."

They're all staring at me like I said I want to sell body parts or something.

Usually, it's easy to get them to go along with things. But now that I'm talking 'bout mopping and dusting, their jaws get tight.

"Why would we wanna be somebody's maid?" Zora asks.

Mai is the next to speak up. "No. No way," she says, curling up her lips and shaking her head. "My mom and dad work me like a dog now. Got me always smelling like grease and chicken and fried pork from working on their food truck. No way am I gonna start smelling like bleach, and Pine-Sol, too." She stands up and starts making fun of her dad. He's Korean. "Egg roll. Yes, we have that . . . and collard greens with a side of fried rice. Yes, yes," she says, smiling way too much, and bowing down low while she wipes her hands on an invisible apron, and pats sweat from her forehead.

"He is so embarrassing," she says. "Always talking that talk. He's been in this country twenty years and he still can't speak English right," she says, throwing a handful of bobby pins across the room.

Mai has a faraway look in her eyes. "Why did my mother have to marry my father? Why not a nice black man like your dad, Zora? He's nice. Smart."

I want to tell Mai to stick to the subject of us making money cleaning houses. But it's too late. Zora's talking about her mom and dad and how she ended up living with her father, not her mother.

Then Ja'nae steps in. "Mai, you lucky you even got a dad," she says. Ja'nae don't even know her father. Not even his name. And her mother just up and left one day. She went to the store for orange juice and cigarettes. Two days later she called to say she was in California, that she had to get her head clear. That was years ago.

Ja'nae's grandmother calls Ja'nae's mother the Triflin' Heifer. "That Triflin' Heifer sent you a letter today," she'll say, right in front of me. "That Triflin' Heifer called and asked how you doing. Like she really care." Ja'nae never says nothing about her mother to her grandmother. But sometimes, when I spend the night at Ja'nae's place, she cries herself to sleep, holding on to letters from that Triflin' Heifer.

CHAPTER SEVEN

I go over to Zora's CD player and put on some tunes. Ja'nae is the first one to start dancing. Her arms and legs are flying all over the place. Mai is singing loud with the music like she can really carry a tune. Zora's foot is moving back and forth inside her sleeping bag. I'm watching all of them jammin' to the music.

When the music stops, I go to Zora's bathroom, stick my mouth underneath the faucet, and take a few gulps. "Y'all with me on this housecleaning thing?" I ask, wiping my mouth dry with the back of my hand.

They don't even bother to answer me. Ja'nae just puts on another CD and starts throwing down again. The harder she dances, the more she sweats, and the sweeter the room gets. Ja'nae got this thing about smelling good. She says kids think all fat people stink. So she makes sure she smells good twenty-four/seven. She's got cotton balls sprayed with perfume pinned to her bra strap, stuffed in her pocket, and sitting in her purse. Sometimes it's too much, and the smell can make you wanna gag.

"The only one that makes any money working with you is you," Mai says, knocking her skinny hips from side to side. Next thing I know, she's at the mirror, frowning, going for her eyebrows with the tweezers. She's pushing up the end of her brow with one finger and holding down her eyelid with another.

Mai's brows are big, bushy, shiny things. They are beautiful, though, just like her slanty eyes, and long, thick lashes. Half the time, people can't figure out what race she is. And they're always telling her how exotic she looks, like she's some kind of bird or plant that somebody shipped here from halfway 'cross the world.

While Mai picks at herself, Zora starts agreeing with her. "Raspberry, we work hard for you and don't get nothing out the deal," Zora says, going over to her drawer and pulling out three crumpled dollar bills. "See." She throws balls of money across the room. One of 'em lands right in Ja'nae's shoe. "Three lousy bucks for all my work."

Ja'nae takes the cash and puts it into her pocket. Zora hunches her shoulders like three dollars ain't no big deal. If somebody threw money at me, I wouldn't be shrugging it off, even if it was a penny.

I can tell by how all three of them are looking that they ain't gonna change their minds. They're fed up with my stuff, same as Momma.

"Old folks would pay big-time for somebody to help 'em out," I say.

"My mother didn't raise no maid," Zora says.

Mai screwed up her eyebrows, but she throws up her shoulders like she could care less. Now she's squeezing a pimple, watching a white, wiggly worm-looking thing ooze out all over. She looks a mess standing there with her messed-up eyebrows and that worm sitting on her cheek.

"I gotta go," Ja'nae says. "I gotta interview Ming for a class paper I'm writing."

Nobody asks Ja'nae what the paper is about, 'cause we know she's gonna tell us even if we don't want to know.

"It's for English class," she says. "Mr. Knight says we should interview somebody we know. Get them to tell us something noteworthy about themselves."

Mai turns around. She got her hands on her hips and her lips stuck out. Her cheek is as red as an apple.

When Zora sees Mai's face, she turns away fast. I know she wanna bust out laughing. But she knows now ain't the time. So she goes and lies down on the bed and shoves a fistful of cheese balls into her mouth.

Mai tells Ja'nae she better not go dragging her business into school. "I'm not playing," Mai says, getting loud.

Next thing I know, Ja'nae is messing with Mai, telling her she and Ming should be proud of being mixed.

"I ain't mixed. I'm black . . . like you," Mai says, throwing her tweezers at Ja'nae.

I don't know why Ja'nae even goes there. She knows how Mai feels about her mixed race, and how Ming feels about being mixed, too. Ming don't want to be called black, African American, or Korean. He says he's biracial. Mai don't want to be called Korean or biracial. She's black. Call her anything different, and she will go off on you.

Ja'nae won't stop talking about her paper for school. She's saying maybe she will even interview Mr. Kim, Mai's dad.

Mai's looking like she wanna hurt somebody. "Why don't you go write about your own screwed-up family," she says, getting up in Ja'nae's face, stomping loud on the floor. Now Zora's dad is yelling upstairs for us to stop making so much noise, to stop acting like hoodlums, and start acting like young ladies.

Ja'nae and Mai get real quiet, but they're still in each other's face.

"You interview my dad, or Ming and I'll . . . I'll . . . I'll tell your grandfather you snuck Ming into your house when he wasn't home."

Ja'nae's eyes get all big. She knows what happens to sneaks in her granddad's house. They get into big-time trouble.

Ja'nae tries to defend herself. "It's not like we did anything. We just watched TV. Anyhow, my grandmother knows about Ming. She was there when he came over."

"So your grandmother gonna get in trouble, too," Mai says, rubbing Vaseline on her eyebrows.

Zora don't seem bothered by none of this. She's just watching it all, lying on her bed, still stuffing her face with cheese balls.

"Forget you and your brother and your whole stupid family," Ja'nae says.

All of a sudden, Zora's making this sound like a cat coughing up hair balls. Soggy, half chewed-up cheese balls come flying out her mouth and all over Ja'nae's feet.

"You *pig*. You did that on purpose," Ja'nae says, shaking her foot, kicking cheese stuff onto Zora's white rug.

Soon Ja'nae's got Zora pressed down on her bed, and she's pouring the can of cheese balls down her shirt. Mai and me grab the can and start bouncing cheese balls off each other's head.

When I look up, there's Zora's mom standing in the doorway. "What's going on here?" she wants to know. "Pick up the mess and keep down the noise, girls," she says, stomping over to the bed, and jerking Ja'nae's hands off Zora.

I want to ask why she even cares what's going on. She ain't living here no more. Her and Zora's dad are divorced, only you wouldn't know it. Her mom comes by a couple times a week and walks around the house like she owns it. Tells the housekeeper what to do, stuff like that.

Zora thinks it's goofy, too. But her parents say they don't want their divorce to change her life.

When Ms. Mitchell turns around to leave, I grab one of the cheese balls and throw it after her. It gets stuck in the back of her hair.

"Somebody thinks they're funny?" she asks, stomping out the room, pulling the cheese ball out her hair. Ja'nae falls down on the bed, laughing, with her hand over her mouth. Zora runs into her bathroom, slams the door, and starts cracking up. I cover my head with a blanket, but I can hear Ms. Mitchell walking down the steps, saying she don't know why we always gotta be hanging out at her child's house. Me, I'm wondering the same thing about her.

CHAPTER EIGHT

The principal put it in writing this time.

Dear Ms. Hill: Your daughter is no longer permitted to sell items in the school. Her entrepreneurial spirit has brought us more than our share of complaints. Just yesterday, three students came to me complaining about something else she had sold them. Two weeks ago, it was the Valentine's Day incident. The next item or items that she brings to sell at Beacon Middle School will result in her suspension. . . .

We're in the car on the way to school again.

The windows are foggy, and it's raining real hard. Momma hands me the letter from the principal. She says she don't wanna get no more letters like this from him. "As of this minute, you are out of business, young lady. That means you ain't—aren't—permitted to sell a thing in school ever again," she says, shaking the letter at me.

I let her know I'm finished with selling things. Then I tell her how me and Zora, Mai, and Ja'nae are gonna clean people's houses to earn money. Momma's face is pressed close to the windshield. Every once in a while, she takes her hand and wipes the glass so she can see better. Our defroster ain't working today, so it's a wonder we ain't crashed into a pole by now.

"You think I'm gonna let you go into some stranger's house and mop up? No way," she says pulling the car over in front of Sato, Kevin, and some other kids. I wipe away the window fog with my coat sleeve. When we pull up to them, Sato and his boys look me dead in the face. I wanna die.

Momma will pick up anybody. She ain't

gonna let somebody she knows stand in the rain for a bus.

"We ain't gonna work for strangers," I say, not really telling the truth. "We gonna work for people we know . . . neighbors, and friends of you and Dr. Mitchell."

I don't get to hear what Momma thinks of my idea. Her mind is fixed on picking up Sato. She puts the car in park, opens the door, and sticks her head out in the rain to tell him and his boys they can ride with us. When she looks over my way she got rain running down her face, and into her mouth. I'm sliding down in the seat again . . . hoping they tell Momma they'd rather take the bus.

But just my luck, Sato's yanking on my door, knocking on my window. He's trying to get me to open up the back door on my side. I shake my head no. "Go around to my mother's side. This side is stuck today."

They squeeze in behind Momma. Four boys with legs long as ironing boards. Not one of 'em carrying a school book, or a book bag. Before they're in the car, I hear one of the kids cracking on our broken rearview mirror, and

Sato's telling Momma she gotta do something about the back seat. "Miz Hill, you can't be going 'round with your seats taped up. It ain't cool, you know."

Momma's laughing right along with 'em. She *should* just pull over and toss 'em out. But no, she's holding a conversation with them about fixing cars. And she's asking how they think they gonna learn something without books.

Naturally, Sato's homework is rolled up like a newspaper in his back pocket. And Kevin says his books are in his locker. Momma believes anything they say. And today they're saying plenty.

"Miz Hill," Sato says, getting close to Momma's ear. "Did you know your daughter's in love?"

I shoot my eyes back at Sato. Wondering why he's making up stuff on me.

Momma plays along. "Is she, Sato? She didn't tell me that. You wanna give me the four-one-one?"

Sato looks at his boys and laughs. "You all right, Miz Hill," he says, shaking his head.

The car pulls up to school, and I'm pushing myself against the door trying to get out. Sato and his crew are cracking up. "Better crawl out the window," he says, making me mad. I don't tell him the window don't work either.

When we all start to get out the car, Momma asks him, "Now who is Raspberry in love with?"

"Oooh. You know she likes old men, really old men," Sato says, digging in his pocket and pretending to pull out some money. "Washington, Lincoln . . ."

Momma covers her mouth, but she's laughing with Sato.

"Can I get out, please?" I say. She opens her door, gets out, and stands in the rain to let me out on her side.

When we get under the awning at the front steps of our school, Sato's still cracking on me. "Pistachio," he says, messing with my name again. "Your mom's ride is messed up." He's got this big, pretty smile on his face. "It needs some serious help." His boys are listening, taking off their wet leathers and saying smart stuff.

"I got some more tape in my locker if she need some to hold her seats together," one of 'em says.

I reach into my pocket and hold tight to my money. "I'm gonna have me a Lexus one day. Y'all won't be laughing then," I say, turning my back on them.

CHAPTER NINE

Ja'nae and Mai are waiting at the door for me as soon as I get inside the building. Ja'nae's got spit on her finger. She's telling Mai to come closer so she can use it to help lay down them wild eyebrows of hers. Mai says she better not put that stuff on her. Ja'nae wipes her finger off on her skirt.

"I gotta talk to you, girl," Ja'nae says to me. Then she tells Mai her brows look funny. Like they painted on or something.

"What?" I say. "Tell me now."

"Later," Ja'nae says, telling Mai she needs to use her own spit on them brows. Mai sticks her finger in her mouth, and traces her brows with it. She tells Ja'nae to get off her case about her eyebrows, but she keeps wiping spit on 'em till the three of us are way down the hall.

We're almost to Mai's locker when Kevin calls Mai over to him. She tells him she ain't got time to talk. That she's going to class. Kevin says, "So?" and keeps waving Mai over his way. After Mai turns him down four times, he yells out real loud, "I don't want no crooked-eyed half-breed—no way." That's when Mai stops, turns around, and stares Kevin down.

Mai is so small that he could fold her up and put her in his pocket if he wanted. But she's all guts, and so she drops her books and goes to him. She don't get in his face, point her finger, or make her head go from side to side like some girls do. She's standing straight and still. She's talking slow and easy. "I'm black, like you," she says.

"Your daddy ain't black," Kevin says under his breath. He won't leave it alone. "That rice walker father of yours ain't black, and neither is you," he says, picking up his books.

Mai's standing there, like she don't know what to do. But she don't want to defend her dad. Shoot, he's the reason she's always being picked on. But she don't want to back down neither. "If you want to know what I am," she says, "look at my nose and my hair, and my skin. Not my mixed-up mom and pops."

Kevin starts to walk away. But he stops a minute to mouth off one more time. "I seen your parents. That's why I know what you *ain't*, no matter what you say you *is*."

Kids are standing around laughing. Me and Ja'nae stick up for Mai, letting cabbage-head Kevin know that he ain't God, and he ain't got the right to say who's what.

Mai is picking up her stuff, holding back tears. Kevin is about to start up again. But Ja'nae says something that ends the whole thing. "Kevin, wasn't the police at your house last week 'cause your mom and dad was fighting on the porch again?" she says, grabbing hold of Mai's arm and pushing her up the hall.

Everybody starts laughing good now. Kevin's trying to say she's lying, making stuff up, which she is. But Mai is our girl. And we ain't gonna let him keep roughing her up with his words.

"You three dingdongs think you smart," Kevin says, acting like he wants to come mess with us some more.

"We *know* we smart," I yell, turning around and making a face at him.

"Hey, Kevin, here's something for your stinking feet," Ja'nae says, throwing one of her cotton balls at him. Then we start running, and we don't stop, even when the principal yells after us to walk like we got good sense.

The four of us ain't in every class together. Just a few. Today Miss Brittle, our math teacher, has to tell us three times to be quiet. We're trying to tell Zora what happened with Kevin. Every time we try, one of us busts out laughing. "Ja'nae, you shut him down good, girl. Shut him down," I say, leaning over to give her five. Mai gives me this funny, fake smile. She knows, like we know, that Kevin's gonna come back saying something else 'bout her. And even if he don't, other kids will. They always do.

When lunchtime comes around, I'm so hungry I break down and buy me some real food. Cheese fries, chicken fingers, and vanilla pudding. Before I can even swallow one bite, Ja'nae comes in the lunchroom, asking to borrow money.

"Money?" I say, hoping she ain't really expecting me to cough up no cash.

"Yeah," Ja'nae says, leaning over and taking a bite out her homemade sandwich. The spiral curl hanging in her eye is swinging back and forth like a rope. The rest of her hair is shooting out the top of her head like a water fountain on high blast.

Ja'nae sticks her tongue out the corner of her lips, and starts drawing on the table with a red pencil short as her baby finger. Next thing you know there's a fat, gray heart on the table, with her and Ming's name in it.

"If I don't get some money quick," she says, "my granddaddy's gonna explode."

Ja'nae's still got her tongue circling her lips like that's helping her draw better. I wanna tell her to keep her tongue in her mouth, but I just listen up. "Last week somebody asked to borrow money from me. She said she'd pay me back. But now she's broke, ain't got a dime. And neither do I."

I'm trying to figure out who Ja'nae lent money to. She only hangs out with me, Mai, and Zora. If she lent one of them money, I'd know about it.

Then Ja'nae fesses up. She says she got ahold of her granddad's stash while he was in the bathroom taking a pee. He's been looking for the missing money ever since. "I told him that he's getting old," she says, "that he probably hid it from hisself, you know? But if he don't find it soon, he gonna start suspecting me."

"You better tell whoever you lent that money to, to give it back," I say, taking that curl from in front of Ja'nae's face and wrapping it behind her ear.

Ja'nae's drawing another heart on the table. I wanna tell her to forget about Ming when he walks into the lunchroom, wearing a new black leather jacket.

I look at Ja'nae, she looks at me, and starts with the stupid hearts again.

Ming don't come over to us, which ain't like him. He stays with Sato and his friends.

They fingering his coat. Slapping him five. Asking how he coughed up the cash to pay for it. Shoot, they know his parents ain't buying leather. They put every penny they make back into their food truck.

"You gotta give me the money, Raspberry," Ja'nae says, moving over one seat to get closer to me. "You know how my granddaddy is. If he don't find that two hundred dollars quick, he's gonna know I took it."

"Two hundred dollars! You crazy?" I say so loud kids at the other end of the table turn and look my way.

"You always gotta be talking about money," Seneca says, walking up to the table and slamming down her books.

I roll my eyes at her. What she know about needing money? She's like Zora. Her parents got big-time jobs. They're both supervisors at the factory across town. She got every kind of coat in the world. Leather. Suede. Silk. Long. Short. Me, I got one—a beat-up pea jacket.

Seneca takes the hint. Next thing you know, she's up in somebody else's face.

"C'mon, Raspberry, if you lend me the

money, I'm gonna give it back," Ja'nae says, looking scared.

Ja'nae just don't get it. I don't even spend my own money on me. I watch money. Count it. Smell it. But I don't spend it. I can't. You spend it, and it's gone. Then you got *nada*, nothing.

Ming finally comes over to our table. He sits down next to Ja'nae and next thing you know, she's cheesing big-time. Rubbing his new leather, asking if he wants some of her lunch.

For ten whole minutes, neither one of 'em speaks to me. They're all up in each other's face, whispering to each other. Ming is playing with a piece of Ja'nae's hair. Ja'nae's got her pinkie finger through the tiny baby ring Ming wears on a chain around his neck. It's real gold. His dad gave him and Mai one when they each turned one year old. It's a Korean custom to give kids gold on their first birthday. Mai keeps her ring in her junk drawer at home.

Ja'nae takes out a pen and writes her name on Ming's hand. Then he writes his name on her arm. All the while, she's rubbing the sleeve of his coat, telling him how nice it feels.

When Ming says, "Thanks for hooking me up," Ja'nae gives him a look that lets him know he needs to shut his mouth.

I can't believe it. We're only thirteen. How can a girl our age give a boy something that expensive? I mean, I know a girl who gave a boy some gloves and a hat for his birthday. But a whole *coat*? No way!

Ming stands up to leave. "See you in Spanish class," he says, walking away.

Ja'nae starts with the money talk again. "Raspberry. You gonna help me out or what? You know my granddad will go off if he finds out I took his money."

"Get it from Ming," I say, throwing my book bag over my shoulder and walking out of the lunchroom.

CHAPTER TEN

Everyone in Ja'nae's house is fat, even the dog. But that don't keep her grandma from cooking all day long. Me, I ain't complaining none. They feed me good. Always send me home with a plate of food so big it lasts Momma and me a few days.

"Everything okay?" Ja'nae's grandma asks. Every time she comes into the room she brings a little something. A pitcher of Kool-Aid. Homemade pound cake. Barbecued chicken wings.

"Do your grandma think of anything besides food?" I ask, hot, spicy barbecue sauce making my fingers stick together and coating my teeth.

"She's from the South. They like to feed people." Ja'nae puts her head back, opens her mouth wide, and stuffs it with lemon pound cake.

Ja'nae and me are trying to figure out this housecleaning thing. Two days ago, I broke down and lent her the money she took from her grandfather. Her granddad was starting to say some really mean things about her. So we agreed that any money Ja'nae earns from cleaning houses is gonna go to me, until she pays back what she borrowed.

When Ja'nae's grandmother comes into her room again, I tell her what we're planning to do. She likes the idea of us helping old people. She says a little hard work won't hurt us none. Now she's sitting on Ja'nae's bed, telling us how she used to clean folks' houses for nearly nothing.

"Gals today can make a nice bit of change if they ain't lazy and do it right. But it's hard work, you know. You gonna earn every dime you make."

Ja'nae looks at me like she wants out already. I turn around and ask her grandmother if she knows anybody that can use our help. Her grandmother twists her lips to the side and shuts her left eye for a minute. "Hmmm. Miss Neeta, next door. She would be a good one, if she'll let you in."

I look at Ja'nae, and she starts laughing.

"What?" I say.

"Nothing," she says laughing again.

"Don't you pay her no mind," Ja'nae's grandma says, lifting herself off Ja'nae's bed. "Miss Neeta's just different is all." She grabs ahold of our plates and cups and starts to leave. She's eyeing the chicken bones, and mumbling how we don't know nothing 'bout eating chicken good. Next thing you know, she got a chicken bone sticking out her mouth. Her tongue and teeth go to work on the little bit of meat still left on the bone.

I don't like it when Ja'nae's granddad takes me home. All he talks about is how bad it is up my way. "Lock your doors now. Don't go staring too hard at folks. I'm too old to fight," he says, soon as I jump in his ride. And for the next ten minutes, he's going off about the loud noise and all the boys hanging out round my neighborhood.

He leaves me off at the bottom of the hill like I ask him to. I tell him I got to pick up some stuff from the truck on the corner. It's the only store we got around here for five whole blocks. But the real reason I wanted to be left off away from my building is to see who's hanging out. When Momma's at work, I'm either at Zora's or I'm in lockdown. Once in a while I just wanna be outside like normal people.

It's chilly out, but not cold enough to keep people inside. Odd Job, a guy who's always trying to make a dollar, is on his usual corner, washing car windows, and talking stuff. He yells my name, and tells his boys they better work it if they want to make some real money tonight.

I turn the corner and wonder how much money he'll take in today.

"What's shaking, Raspberry?" says Eva Jones, Sato's cousin.

"Nothing," I say, checking my watch to see what time it is. Momma's gonna call me in twenty minutes to see if I'm home yet.

I sit down on the cracked, cold steps. Every word coming out of Eva's mouth is funny. She's busting on her momma, bad. Talking about the principal and his long, skinny head. She's on everybody's case. Next thing you know, here comes Sato. Eva don't cut him no slack neither. She starts jumping all over him. Talking about his coat sleeves being too short, and his feet too long and flat. When she says that, I tuck my feet under my book bag so she don't start riding my case next.

Ten minutes before Momma's set to call, I head for home. Sato says he's gonna walk with me. Eva says she always knew he liked me. He tells her to shut up.

Sato ain't his usual big-mouth self. He's quiet tonight. He don't even make fun of my name or nothing. It's nice. And for once I don't feel like a knucklehead liking somebody who clearly don't like me.

When we're almost to my place, Sato starts talking. Telling me that his aunt, Eva's mom, borrowed some money from his parents and he had to bring it over to her.

He's asking me about homework, and talking about Ming's new coat.

"That coat's nice. Real nice," he says, leaning against the wall of my building like he's planning to stay awhile. I smell his cologne, and his sweat. I would never tell Zora and Ja'nae and Mai, but it smells good, all mixed up together.

I grab hold of the thick metal door handle and put my key in the lock.

"Your mom at work?" Sato says, like he's trying to keep me from going in.

"Always," I say, pulling open the door, the smell of pee filling my nose.

I can hear the phone ringing down the hall. I know it's Momma checking in on me. I turn to Sato to say good night. He starts talking about something else. Looking right in my eyes when he's saying it, too. For a minute, I swear I can't breathe. Sato's too close. Smelling too good. Looking too fine.

After ten rings, the phone stops. Then it starts ringing all over again. "Bye, Sato," I say, not turning to leave.

Sato looks into my face with them eyes of

his. I swallow hard. I tell my feet to get going. But they don't budge. And my heart don't slow down when I tell it to neither.

All of a sudden, I hear somebody calling my name. "Raspberry sodaaa!" It's Shoe talking loud. He got his head stuck out the window, and he's pouring a cup of water out the window right over Sato's head. Check is there, too.

"You in trouble, girl," Shoe says like he's happy. "You know you supposed to be inside by dark."

"Yeah, Raspberry syrup," Check says, telling me to watch out, 'cause he wants to see how long his spit will take to hit the ground.

"I gotta go," I say, turning my back to Sato.

"Later," he says, walking off. Check and Shoe's spit just misses Sato's head.

"I'm gonna tell on you two," I say, stomping up the steps.

Before I can get my key in the lock, their grandmother is at her door, yelling down at me. Saying I know better than to be coming in late. She's talking about how she promised Momma to look out for me at night. I finally open the door, grab hold of the phone, and listen to Momma yelling at me in one ear, and at the same time, listening to Shoe's grandma hollering at me for leaving the key in the lock and the door wide open. I ain't paying neither one of them no mind. I'm thinking about Sato, and how warm I felt inside when he smiled at me like he did.

CHAPTER ELEVEN

As soon as we walk into Miss Neeta's place, I know Ja'nae and me got a lot of work ahead of us. Miss Neeta is a pack rat. She never throws nothing out. In her living room, she got old newspapers piled in stacks up to the ceiling. The kitchen ain't no better— there's dirty Styrofoam cups with black coffee rings on the ironing board, and circling a dead plant on the kitchen table.

You name it, Miss Neeta's got it. Boxes. Books. Shoes. Dirt. A thousand pieces of used foil are sitting on top her television. I want to cry.

"My grandma's been wanting to get in here and clean since forever," Ja'nae whispers.

"I wish your grandma was here now,"
I say.

Ja'nae introduces me to Miss Neeta, a little
old woman with blue eyes, faded purple hair,
and yellow fingernails. She says everything
twice. "Come in. Come in. Sit down. Sit
down."

Miss Neeta lets us know that she don't let
just anyone touch her things. "But with me
getting up in years, I need a little help right
about now," she says.

She looks at us without blinking. "I'm
testing you. Testing you now, you hear. First,
I will see how well you clean the living room
over there." She points, like we're too stupid
to figure out which room is the living room.
"If you do okay, I'll give you more work.
If you screw up, no second chances. None."

I take a deep breath and I check out Miss
Neeta's curtains, which look older than she is.
Even the air smells old in this place. I want to
tell Ja'nae I'm out of here. But then I think of
the money, and I keep my mouth shut.

Ja'nae's grandma is smart. Before we left
to come here, she gave us rubber gloves, a

bucket, a broom, and an extra-large box of soap powder. "There's more where this come from," she said.

We been cleaning for a hour and a half, but hardly make a dent. "There ain't enough soap powder in the world to clean this joint," I tell Ja'nae. I wipe my forehead with my arm. I'm sweating all over.

It would help if Miss Neeta would leave us alone. But every fifteen minutes she's in the living room checking our work and talking.

"So how's school?" she wants to know. "You get good grades?"

I'm thinking if I lie and tell her that I am an A student, she'll stop talking. The truth is I get mostly B's. Ja'nae gets A's all the time.

Lying about my grades don't help. Miss Neeta keeps talking. She eases herself down in the chair. "Hard work is good for you," she says. "Very good." She goes on and on about how much she worked when she was a little kid. When she finally heads for the kitchen, I throw a wet sponge at Ja'nae.

"Girl, we gonna be here all night," I say.

Ja'nae throws the sponge back at me.

"Ain't she messy. Man, we could make a million dollars just cleaning this place," Ja'nae says, rearranging the flower she brought for Miss Neeta. "No matter how messy a place is, flowers make it look like someplace special," Ja'nae says. I don't see how no tiny flower gonna make a difference here. There's too much mess for that little thing to do any good.

Finally, three and a half hours later, we're close to finished. It don't look like we did much, though. There's still two baskets in the corner piled high with clothes and a bunch of busted-up shoes underneath the table.

"Miss Neeta, you need to throw some of this old stuff out," I finally say.

Ja'nae hits me in the side with her elbow, then shakes her head quick like Momma does when she wants me to shut my big mouth.

"I never throw things away. Never. No, sir," Miss Neeta says. She opens the door to see us out. "I will see you again next week."

I look at Ja'nae. Ja'nae looks at me. We walk over to the door.

I give the place a final look before we're

about to leave, and I can see we done that place some good. The cracked mirror is shining. The wood around it looks like you could ice-skate on it. I can see the rug now, which was covered with pieces of string from all the sewing Miss Neeta does.

Miss Neeta is smiling. Next thing I know, she's yanking up her dress. Showing us her big old girdle. She grabs a hold of the garter belt that's holding up her runny stockings, uncurls the money tucked inside, and shoves a fifty-dollar bill in Ja'nae's hand, and a fifty-dollar bill in mine!

"You come back next Wednesday. Next Wednesday afternoon," she says.

I nod and lick my lips. I stare at Ja'nae, then back at the money. I eyeball Miss Neeta, and rub the fifty-dollar bill over and over again. "I love making money," I holler. "I just love it!"

CHAPTER TWELVE

"Pay up," I tell Ja'nae, when we get outside onto Miss Neeta's porch. I don't mean to be so cold-blooded, but business is business.

Ja'nae puts down her empty cleaning bucket and stands shivering in the cold. Neither one of us is wearing a coat. "I know I still owe you money," she says, squinting at the clouds blocking the sun up in the sky, "but I can't pay you nothing today. I'll give you back some of what I owe you next time we clean houses. Okay?"

I kick that stupid bucket and send it flying into the wooden banister separating Miss Neeta's porch from Ja'nae's. The wet rags spill all over the porch. "See, this is why I don't lend people money. They get all funny on you when it's time to pay up," I say, picking up the rags, and slapping them into the bucket.

"I'll pay you back, Raspberry. But I can't give you none of today's money. I need it for something." Ja'nae swings one leg over the banister, then parks her big butt down on the banister like she's riding a horse. She's got one foot on each porch now. "I'm *not* trying to get over on you, Raspberry," she's whining.

I don't say a word to Ja'nae when we get inside her house. She's showing off her money to her grandmother, putting it down on the table, in between the salt and pepper shakers. She says she's putting it in the bank tomorrow.

"Let me heat you up some tea," her grand-mother says, setting cups and saucers down in front of me and Ja'nae.

Ja'nae's grandmother tells Ja'nae to come help her get the leftover chicken out of the basement freezer. "Watch the teapot," she says to me.

I'm sitting there, watching the money, not the teapot. Next thing I know, that fifty bucks is in my pocket, and the teapot is blowing steam and whistling real loud, like it's telling on me.

My fingers are still in my pocket when her grandfather comes into the room.

"You two made out all right at Neeta's, huh?" Ja'nae's grandfather says, turning down the flame under the teapot.

"Yeah," I say. I pick up the salt shaker, sprinkle salt in my hand, and lick it off.

"James, we can't get this chicken unstuck," Ja'nae's grandmother yells up from the basement.

She's gotta call him three more times before he goes downstairs to help out.

I'm rubbing the money in my pocket. Telling myself that it's okay to take what people owe you if they're too selfish to give you what's yours. So while they're all in the basement trying to get the chicken, I put on my coat, throw my backpack over my shoulder, and walk out the door with my money.

It's dark and cold outside. I push my hands down in my coat pocket, and walk down the steps. The Wilsons are still in the basement. I can see their shadows through the thin yellow curtains.

I don't make it past Miss Neeta's house before I stop, unfold the fifty-dollar bill, and stare at it under the streetlight. I sit down on Miss Neeta's steps and think about what I just did.

"You belong to me," I say, pushing the money back into my pocket. The cold wind on my face feels like pushpins digging my skin, so I put my head down in my lap and cover my face. When we lived in the streets, Momma would try to make me warmer by pulling me close, wrapping her arms around me, and laying her head on mine. It didn't really do all that much good, but when you living on the streets, you do what you gotta do. Like I gotta take the money. It's mine. And I can't walk home and leave what's mine behind. If I did, where would I be? On the streets again, sure 'nuff.

I pull the money out again and wonder if Ja'nae and her grandparents know I'm gone with her cash. I hold the fifty up by one end and watch it blow in the wind like a flag.

Ja'nae owes me four of these. So why shouldn't I take one of 'em now? I think.

"Raspberry! Raspberry!" Ja'nae screams out her front door. "Where you at, girl?" she yells.

I jump off Miss Neeta's steps and run before Ja'nae starts in on me.

"Raspberry!" she calls again. Before she shuts the door, I'm standing under the street light on the corner, covering my face from the cold. Ja'nae can be such a crybaby, I think to myself. She's probably in the house now boohooing all over the place. "So?" I say, blowing into my hands, trying to heat them up. "Let her cry."

When I think about the time, and how Momma's gonna get next to me for coming in late again, I start running home. I don't stop for three whole blocks. When I do, I'm breathing so hard I feel light-headed. But that don't keep me from thinking about Ja'nae. "She is such a baby," I say, holding my breath so that my heart will slow down some.

I know I should go home. I got a test coming up, and homework to do. And besides,

Momma is probably ringing the phone off the hook. But the more I think about Ja'nae, the worse I feel. I mean, we girls. Last year, when Momma broke her ankle, Ja'nae's grandmother cooked a week's worth of food and gave it to us. Even slipped Momma ten dollars.

So? I think, picking up my pace again. But before I know it, I'm standing still under another streetlight. Wondering if Ja'nae's granddad is yelling at her for being stupid enough to leave the money out. He'll start in on her grandmother, too. Then he'll bring up Ming and they'll be arguing half the night. I turn around and head back to Ja'nae's. The whole time I'm walking back there, part of me is saying to forget about that girl, and to keep the money for myself. The next thing I know, I'm ringing the doorbell.

Ja'nae peeks out the window, then opens the door wide to let me in. She don't ask me why I did what I did. I don't try to explain. I just hand her the money. She folds it up and stuffs it in her back pocket. When we're almost to the kitchen, she turns around and smiles.

"You could never do nothing really wrong," she whispers, picking a bottle of perfume off the table and spraying herself. I close my eyes when she sprays it on me. We walk into the kitchen smelling like peaches.

CHAPTER THIRTEEN

When Momma tiptoes into our place, and comes into my room to check on me and kiss me good night, I act like I'm asleep. I don't need no more lectures, especially at midnight. I know she's mad at me for not calling to tell her I was home as soon as I got in tonight, but that don't keep her from kneeling down by my bed and praying for me, like she does every night.

When Momma's back in the kitchen, I kick off the covers and reach for the sucker I started yesterday. I hear the kitchen radio, and a chair scraping the floor when she pulls it out. I smile when I hear Momma slam her books down on the table, just the way I do when I

79

really don't want to study. Momma's talking to herself now. Reading her work out loud. Telling herself not to fall asleep. Then the phone rings, and she seems wide awake. She's laughing. Talking all proper.

"I am *never* too tired to speak to you," she says. She's talking to Dr. Mitchell.

I grab my can of money from behind my dresser and dump the bills onto the floor. I count my cash while I listen in on Momma and the doctor. This is the only way I'll know what's really going on with them two.

Soon, it's two o'clock in the morning, and Dr. Mitchell's still talking to Momma. I'm thinking, Shoot, I wouldn't want some sleepy doctor prescribing me no pills after he's been up all night gabbing on the phone with some woman. I feel my eyes burning, and closing shut no matter how hard I try to make 'em stay open. I pull out a sock full of change and start counting that, too. At three o'clock, when I take myself to bed, I can still hear Momma laughing.

I wake up screaming. Crying and screaming

so loud that Shoe bangs on his floor upstairs and tells me to shut my big mouth. Momma yells for him to mind his own business. Then she holds me tight for a long time, even after I tell her I'm okay. Even after I tell her about my stupid dream.

In the dream, we're back on the streets. This time, we ain't in a van. We're walking up and down the streets pushing a cart. Begging. Always begging people for something.

The weird thing is that in the dream, I have money. I have a whole cart full of cash, but nobody lets me use it to buy anything. So I just push the cart around, and beg somebody to take the money. To let me use it to get some food, or a house, or a ride somewhere. But everybody keeps shaking their heads and saying, "Your money ain't no good here."

Momma don't say a word when I tell her about my dream. While I'm talking, I remember that Dr. Mitchell, Sato, and Zora were in my dream, too. They turned away my money like everyone else in the dream. And when I showed Dr. Mitchell all the money I had, he just laughed and said it wasn't enough. "Not enough for what?" I asked. He said, "It's just not enough. It won't ever be enough."

Later, on the way to school, Momma tells me that good things are finally going to happen to us. She's all excited when she tells me she got another part-time job.

My face gets hot. "I never see you now," I say, looking at her like she's lost her mind. I remind her that she's taking two classes at the university. That when she ain't in school, she's writing papers and trying to figure out math problems, or working, or getting ready to go to work. She's trying to explain that she's doing this for me—for us.

"We don't see each other now," I say. "We do everything together in this stupid, broke-down car," I say, slapping the taped-up rearview mirror. "We go over my homework in the car. Make up grocery lists in the car. Write notes to teachers in the car. We might as well be sleeping in here, too, like we did in the van," I snap.

Momma gets real quiet. I stare out the window so I don't have to look at her. When she turns the corner, our tires go up on the curb. A woman standing at the bus stop points at us, and curses Momma out.

I start counting in my head the number of blocks we got till we get to school.

We're almost there when Momma tells me something she thinks will make things better. We're moving out of the projects, but she ain't saying where or when.

She looks at me. "That's why I need this other job. So I can have enough money to put a security deposit down on the house. To buy stuff we need for it. Curtains. New dishes. Bedspreads. Stuff like that."

I don't know, maybe I shouldn't care if Momma gotta work another gig long as we're getting a new house out of this. But then I think, all her working is only gonna get us a bigger place for me to be by myself in.

Momma's going on and on about the new job, and our new place. But I'm wondering, how many jobs does it take for her to make enough money for us to live good? Too many, I guess.

CHAPTER FOURTEEN

Ja'nae's got a big mouth. She told Zora and Mai about me taking the money. She said she wasn't trying to say I was a thief. Just that I was the kind of person who couldn't do wrong no matter how hard I tried. Zora and Mai don't see it that way, though. They say I'm straight up wrong for what I did, and they think Ja'nae is crazy for forgiving me.

"I might have to search you the next time you leave my house," Zora says, sounding like she's serious.

I give Ja'nae the evil eye. She tries to apologize. "I didn't mean nothing by it," she says.

"Well, if you didn't mean nothing, why'd you tell?" I say, getting mad at her.

Mai is walking by us, shaking her head. "Why'd you take Ja'nae's money, then?" she asks me.

"It was stupid, all right?" I snap. "But she owes me money. Plenty of it," I say. "Still does."

Ja'nae tells everyone that they're missing the point. "A real thief don't give you back nothing. They keep on rolling. A real friend don't do you wrong. Raspberry proved she was a real friend," she says.

Zora's eyes are the color of sand today. They make her look weird, like somebody on *Star Trek*. She makes a sucking sound with her teeth and says, "Ja'nae told me how much money you two got for cleaning that old lady's house. Next time you go to clean, count me in," she says, kicking a balled-up piece of paper out of her way.

"I still need sixty dollars to buy sneakers. If I can't pay my half, my father won't let me get them. And I really need those sneakers. They go with a new outfit my mother just bought me."

Ja'nae sees Ming and starts waving

him over. She tells Zora that all she needs to do is work with us two times and she'll be able to pay the costs of her half of the sneakers, plus have some money left over.

We change the subject when Ming walks up. Right away he starts rubbing Ja'nae's cheeks with his hands. She's smiling all over the place. Ming's saying he's gonna walk Ja'nae home before he goes to his parents' food truck. Mai's right behind Ja'nae and her brother, complaining about working the food truck. But Ming ain't paying Mai no attention. He's got his arm wrapped around Ja'nae's shoulder, telling her how good she smells.

After school, Zora and me are outside the building, talking, when Momma pulls up to the curb and tells us to get in. "I'll drive you home, Zora," Momma says, handing me a pack of gum. I give two sticks to Zora. I stack three sticks together like a sandwich and bite down.

When we pass Zora's street, we tell Momma that she needs to turn the car around. But Momma ain't listening. A few minutes later, she stops the car in front of somebody else's house. The brick house is the color of warm milk with a hunk of butter in it. The roof is shaped like a dunce cap. A faded white picket fence goes all the way around.

"Who you know live here?" I ask, getting out the car on Momma's side.

"You like?" Momma asks me. She turns to Zora with the same question in her eyes.

"I guess," Zora says, frowning at the mess in the front yard, and in the alleyway. Three old tires are sitting on the lawn by the tree, right next to a rusted bathroom sink. The window shades are rusty, too, and they've got giant pieces missing from them. The paint on the front door and around the windows is cracked and peeling.

"We—we're—gonna be living here, I hope," Momma says, following me onto the porch.

Zora and me look at each other. We can't afford a new paint job for our car, how we gonna afford a house? I think.

Momma sticks her face up to the window and looks inside. I look, too. The place has wooden floors, nice ones. A kitchen counter with tall, wooden stools. A fake fireplace. But still, it needs a paint job real bad. And them rusted blinds and torn-up shades gotta go.

When we're back in the car, Momma explains that she's trying to get a Section 8 so we can move in this messed-up house. She says that the last family who lived here got evicted. "They trashed the place. The neighbors put up a fuss and got them kicked out. But it'll be fixed up real nice before we move in."

Zora ain't hip to Section 8, so she asks all kinds of questions. By the time we get to her house, Momma's still trying to set her straight.

"Section Eight is the government's way of making it possible for people, poor people like us, to move into nice places at cheaper rates," Momma explains. "We pick out a house or apartment we like, and the government pays part of the rent every month. We pay the other part of it. A small part."

Momma starts to get out of the car with Zora. "You don't have to walk me in, Miz Hill," Zora says, trying to pull down her skirt and get out the car at the same time.

But Momma keeps going. When she's halfway up the front walk, she turns back to me and says, "Come on."

Zora looks at her, then at me. She's as confused as I am.

When I'm out the car, Momma says to Zora, "Your father invited us to supper."

That's when it hits me. Momma and Dr. Mitchell got a thing going on between them. And, just like that, everything's clear. Momma ain't trying to get a house for me. She wants this house so she can get closer to Dr. Mitchell.

Zora looks at Momma real suspicious-like when she opens the door and lets us inside.

Dr. Mitchell is standing at the door. He reaches for Momma's coat and kisses Zora on the cheek at the same time.

Momma rubs her cold hands together. "Nice place," she says.

We all walk into the kitchen. Dr. Mitchell dumps wet, hot spaghetti into a strainer. He turns his face from the steam rushing at him. "Dinner's in thirty minutes. You girls can go upstairs and relax in Zora's room until we're ready to eat," he says.

When we get upstairs, Zora slams her bedroom door shut behind us. Her finger is stuck in my face. "What's up with your mother?"

I push her finger aside and lie down on her bed. I pick up one of her old dolls and start playing with her hair. "What?" I say.

"Why is she trying to move here to Pecan Landings, trying to make my father like her?"

I'm sitting with the doll's stringy hair in my lap, trying to think of something that will hurt Zora as much as she's trying to hurt me. "My mother wouldn't want your dad, anyhow. He's a wimp. Dr. Wimp." I make my hand like a microphone. "Dr. Wimp, please come to the emergency room," I'm saying.

"Well, at least my father is taking care of me," Zora says, fixing her sandy eyes on me like she's trying to beam me right back to the projects. "At least he's not some dope addict living in a crack house someplace," she says.

I sit there real quiet, twisting the doll's hair around my finger, not saying nothing.

"Sorry," Zora says after a few minutes. "I shouldn't have said that."

I'm still twisting the doll's hair around my

finger, not looking Zora's way at all.

The whole time, I'm wondering if Zora thinks what I think: What does somebody like Dr. Mitchell want with somebody like Momma, who lives in projects . . . who comes from nowhere?

"Your mother doesn't really like my dad, does she?" Zora asks.

"Not that much, I guess."

Zora shakes her head up and down. We are thinking the same thing. "I don't care really," she says. "But my mother, you know . . ."

I rub the doll's eyelashes. They feel like toothbrush bristles against my finger.

"My mom and dad, they could get back together, you know," Zora says.

I feel sorry for Zora then. I know my mother and father ain't never getting back together. Knowing that makes it easier. You don't spend your time crying over something you know won't ever happen.

"If your parents were getting back together, I would know," I say. "Momma tells me everything," I say, knowing full well that things with Momma and me ain't like they used to be. That Momma's got secrets she don't tell me nothing about.

Zora says, "I don't have nothing against your mom, for real I don't." She gets up when her dad calls us to dinner. "It's just, my mom . . ." she says, taking the doll from me and putting it back on the bed. "I have to look out for my mom, you know?"

Zora reaches her arm out to pull me up from the bed.

I look straight at Zora. "Does your dad love your momma, Zora?" I ask.

Zora takes a breath. "No. Not no more."

"But your momma still loves your dad?" I ask, heading downstairs.

"No—I don't know—maybe. My mom's used to my dad. Like your mom's used to that raggedy car of hers," she says, straightening a picture of Martin Luther King on the wall.

I don't tell her that Momma would get rid of that old junker in a minute if she could afford something better.

At dinner, Momma is talking and smiling and asking me and Zora stuff about school. The usual words that come out her mouth ain't good enough for this place. So all her "ain'ts" are turning to "are nots." She's making her "y'alls" into "you all." Tonight, every word Momma says that would just be fine in the projects gets all dressed up and made into something more dignified and elegant.

At first, I get mad at Momma trying to act all proper. I want to say something to really embarrass her good. But then I see Dr. Mitchell handing her the creamer for her coffee. Asking if she wants some fresh Parmesan cheese for her spaghetti. Pouring her some wine in one of his fancy glasses. And looking at her like she's special. Beautiful. The way I wish Sato would look at me. So I keep my mouth shut.

CHAPTER FIFTEEN

The day before we're supposed to go clean for Miss Neeta again, Miss Neeta calls me and says she made a mistake. She paid us too much money for cleaning her place. Losers weepers, I'm thinking. Then Miss Neeta starts talking about how she has to hold off on paying her gas bill, because her money is short. And how she can't use her lights so she can save on electricity.

I want to say, "Dag, you act like you gave us a thousand dollars." But Miss Neeta's on a fixed income. Her money is tight. I hold my tongue. "How much you want back, Miss Neeta?" I ask, hoping she will just get off the phone.

"You girls did such a nice job," she says.

"You can keep ten, ten dollars each."

Ten dollars for all that work. For lugging boxes, and sniffing dust, and almost breaking my neck on top of a ladder. Ain't no way, lady, I say in my head. Then I tell her I'll talk it over with Ja'nae.

When Ja'nae and I talk it through, I realize I never should have bothered mentioning it to her in the first place. Ja'nae tells her grandmother, who says we should clean Miss Neeta's house out of the goodness of our hearts. No way. I don't work for free. So, we give Miss Neeta fifteen dollars back and tell her we can't clean for her no more.

Ja'nae's grandmother says she knows somebody else looking to hire us. I tell Ja'nae I ain't listening to her grandmother no more. But when she says the person owns an elderly care home, and don't mind spending money, I straighten up. "We can give your grandmother one more chance, I guess," I say, thinking about all the money we can make.

At school, Zora acts like she's mad at me. She don't invite me over to her house or nothing.

I'm thinking it's 'cause of my mom and her dad. I guess she don't like what's happening no more than I do.

For the next few days I stay clear of Zora. But going straight home to an empty place ain't my thing. So today I go with Mai to her folks' food truck. It's parked a few blocks from school. That way, her parents get kids from our school, the college crowd, and the high schoolers two blocks away. Mai is embarrassed working on that food truck. She's got to serve food to the same kids she sits next to in class all day. And she's got to hear them make fun of her dad's English, or her mother's weight.

To make matters worse, kids is always loudmouthing her dad.

"This ain't the right change," Jo Jo Miller says to Mr. Kim.

Mr. Kim takes the money and counts it out for Jo Jo again. "Right," he says. "Here is the quarter I owe you."

"Y'all always trying to get over on us," Jo Jo says, walking away.

Mai's mother goes over to Mr. Kim. She rubs his back with her soft brown hands, and says something to him in Korean.

"English. Speak English!" Mai yells, rubbing her eye. "And you ain't even Korean," she snaps at her mom. "Why you talking that talk?"

Mai can speak and understand Korean, too. When she was little, her dad took her and Ming to a Korean church for language lessons. But after a few weeks, the man who ran the place asked him not to bring them back. Said they didn't fit in. After that, Mr. Kim taught them at home. Mai says he just wasted his time. She ain't never gonna speak a word of that stuff.

Mai's really got an attitude now. She puts on her headphones and turns up the music on her CD player.

Something happens to Mai when she's around her parents. She gets so mean.

Mr. Kim is a proud man. A nice man. He wouldn't hurt or cheat anybody. But the kids around here are just plain mean to him. Mai don't treat her father no better. But she checks herself when she's around Ming, 'cause he don't play that.

Ming got his leather coat open, and an apron hanging from his neck. He's standing by his father. When someone orders rice and vegetables with hot sauce, or black bean sauce and noodles, like the next guy in line, Ming repeats their order in Korean. "One *bibimbap* and *chajang* mein," he says, grabbing a piece of corn bread and a napkin and sticking it in the bag along with the order.

"Don't forget the collard greens. He ordered collard greens, too," his dad says, counting out change for the man.

Ming scoops up a big spoonful of collards and stuffs it in a cup. When Ming turns his back, I stick my finger in the pot of greens, and sneak a piece of bacon. The red pepper flakes his mom uses in the greens burn my lips.

"One *mandu*," Ming says, scooping up some dumplings, "and three *dak jims*," he says, heading for the chicken stew with potatoes. Next he's taking orders for sweet-potato pie and black-eyed peas.

Mai rolls her eyes at Ming. That's when some kids from school walk up. Mr. Kim starts speaking in English, then ends in Korean.

"English! English! Speak English!" Mai says again.

Mr. Kim waits on his customers. Mrs. Kim grabs Mai by the arm and whispers something in her ear. Mai starts yelling. "I will not apologize to him," she says pointing at her dad. "He—you—should apologize to *me*. Everybody's laughing at me 'cause of you two with your Afro-Asian, collard-green, black-eyed-peas, fortune-cookie truck, and your mixed-up kids. Why didn't you two each marry your own kind?" Mai grabs her book bag and coat and heads for the front of the truck. She sits down in the driver's seat, and folds her arms tight across her chest.

Mr. Kim is counting out change to the next customer. Ming takes off his jacket, rolls up his sleeves, and helps his father serve people. Mai's mother hands me a bowl of fried rice and an egg roll busting open with fried cabbage, bacon, and shrimp. "Sit. Eat," she tells me.

Mai's parents are used to her going off. They ignore her, let her cool down. I kick back and eat my egg roll. Mr. Kim hands me an orange soda and some barbecue chicken.

He and his wife are like Ja'nae's grandmother. They will feed you until you explode.

Ten people come up to the truck in the next fifteen minutes. Mr. Kim is scooping, bagging, and handing things off quick as you please. And just when they think things are slowing down, here comes trouble. Kevin, from school.

"You seen a dog 'round here?" he says, walking up to the truck.

Mr. Kim shakes his head.

"You musta seen it," he says, getting louder. "A little bitty thing. Black, with a white patch over his eye. Long haired . . . a mutt, you know," he says, sounding serious. But I see him shooting his eyes back at his boys over there by the tree, and I know a joke is coming.

Mr. Kim don't get it, but Ming does. So does Mrs. Kim. "Y'all get outta here. Get," she says, waving a spatula round like she's gonna smack them.

"Let me . . ." Kevin's laughing so hard he can't get the words out. "Let me check out what you got cooking. I wanna see if you ain't trying to pass my pooch off for chicken," he finally says. His boys can't take it no more.

They rolling all over the bus-stop bench laughing. Telling Kevin he's crazy.

Some people in line behind Kevin make a face, and head for the pizza truck up the street. Ming throws his leather jacket off so fast, a sleeve lands in the rice. He's off the truck hitting Kevin upside the head. Before you know it, Mr. Kim is out there grabbing Ming by the shoulder.

"You can't beat down ignorance with your fists," he says.

Ming is still yelling at Kevin, but he's following his dad back to the truck.

"Ignore them," his mother says, handing Ming a Pepsi.

Kevin and his crew stand by the tree making barking sounds. And saying, "Here doggy, doggy."

Mai's so quiet, I figure maybe she don't hear nothing with her earphones on. But she does hear, and the next thing I know, she jumps from the truck, and heads down the street and around the corner. She don't even have no coat on.

I grab Mai's coat and go after her. I yell and

yell for her to wait for me. She keeps running. I don't try to keep up after a while. I walk at a normal pace. I figure when she gets too cold she'll stop and get her stuff. By the time she stops, we're almost to her house. Her nose is red and runny. Her hands are so cold she can't unbend them to get her keys out. I unlock her front door and help her with her things once we get inside.

It ain't too long before she's feeling all right. After a while, she bad-mouthing her folks.

"You going back on the truck today?" I ask.

"No," Mai says, pushing up her sleeves. She got a bunch of dishes sitting in the sink, with steaming hot water running over 'em. "I'm tired of the doggy jokes. And the cracks about my dad cheating people, and the stuff about how fat my mother is," she says, almost crying.

"Your parents are cool, Mai. You know that," I tell her.

Mai wipes her face with the back of her wet hands. Now she got a big soap bubble hanging from her nose. "I wish they never got married," she says, walking into the living room and sitting down on the couch.

I sit down beside her, put my feet up on the coffee table, and check out the room. There's some of everything in here. African masks. Watercolor paintings of Korea, and a painting of Mai and Ming when they were babies. In the picture, Ming is sitting on his mother's lap. Mai is smiling, and sitting on her father's lap. Her tiny finger is holding tight to his big thumb.

"You look a lot like your dad, only darker," I say, staring at the picture, then back at Mai again.

Mai grabs a handful of her thick, wavy black hair and pulls it away from her face.

"I look like myself," she says, turning away from the painting. "Not nobody else. Just me."

CHAPTER SIXTEEN

The Heifer called. Ja'nae is giving us all the details. She says she talked to her mother all night long, under the covers, so her grandparents couldn't hear. The house was real hot, she said. And even though Ja'nae sweated out her hair, and had to wash under her arms when she was done, she says it was worth it. Ja'nae is talking so fast and so much at lunchtime that she don't get a chance to eat her fries before they go cold.

Ja'nae is telling us all about how her mother's got some job laying hands on sick people. Zora looks at Ja'nae sideways, like she's crazy. But I know all about that hand-laying stuff. On the street it happens a lot. People touching you where it hurts. Your foot. A cut hand. A bad back. And praying for it to get better. Only nobody ever makes no money from laying hands. I guess Ja'nae's mom ain't making much money from it, either. Ja'nae says she's living in somebody's basement, till she builds up her practice.

This is the most Ja'nae has ever said about her mom. And the more she talks, the more we see how much she's been holding back from us. Ja'nae says she talks to her mom almost every night. She uses calling cards to sneak and call her when her grandparents go to bed. Zora asks how she even knew where to find her mother. "I didn't," Ja'nae says, "I picked up the phone one day about two months ago to call Raspberry, and she was on the line trying to phone me. It was weird," she says, shaking her head like she still can't believe it. "We been talking every night since. She wants me to come live with her."

I'm looking at her like she lost her mind. Wondering how she figures her mother can take care of her if she's living off somebody else and trying to make a living doing something that nobody's willing to pay for.

Ja'nae is still talking when Ming walks over and sits down next to her. He's wearing the leather jacket. Sato is with him. He's dressed in all black, from his wave cap to his sneakers. He looks like a gangbanger.

"Hey, greedy," he says, popping me on the head with his rolled-up paper. "Hey, y'all," he says to everybody else.

I ignore him. But deep down I hope he keeps saying stuff to me . . . even if it ain't all that nice.

"Heard you got kicked off the food truck, Mai," Sato says, taking one of Zora's fries. Zora smacks Sato's hand and tells him to stay out of her food.

"My parents say I don't have to work if I don't want."

"That's 'cause you're mean. And don't do no work," Ming says, moving closer to Ja'nae.

Mai rolls her eyes at him. "Forget you," she says, getting up. She walks over to Sato's side of the table, sits down next to him, and says, "I didn't get kicked off of that smelly truck, I quit."

"Shoot," Sato says. "If I quit like that, my mother would knock me upside the head and tell me I had to work anyhow," he says, smacking a plastic fork against the table, then using it to eat his applesauce.

Mai makes this real ugly face at Sato.

Then Sato says what we're all thinking. "You just don't want to be around your dad."

We look at Mai to see what she's gonna say to that.

"Mind your own business," she says. She stands up and grabs her backpack. Ming says something to Mai in Korean. Mai starts to leave. "You only do that to embarrass me," she says, smacking him on the back.

Ja'nae starts whispering something in Ming's ear. Zora holds up a plastic fork like it's a knife she's gonna stick in Sato's hand if he don't let loose on that fry he just took off her plate.

Sato's complaining about still being hungry. I see this as a way to pull in some extra cash. I dig in my backpack and pull out ten bags of barbecue chips.

"Now that's what I call real food," Sato

says, reaching for a bag.

"Real food ain't free," I tell him.

He shakes his head. "Cheap. Greedy and cheap," he says, digging in his pocket and throwing two quarters on the table.

Zora, Mai, and Ming give me money, too, and before I get up from the table, six other kids buy the rest of the chips.

On the way to Spanish class, Ja'nae asks if I can lend her more money. I look at her like she's crazy. "No way! Pay me what you owe me and maybe *then* we can talk," I say, pushing open the door to class.

If Ja'nae paid me everything she owes me plus interest, I wouldn't lend her no more money. But I can't help but wonder why she always got her hand out for money these days.

CHAPTER SEVENTEEN

W e're at Zora's house again. Her mother says she's gonna start charging us rent since we come here so often. I think to myself, Dr. Mitchell need to be charging *you* rent, much as you hang out here.

Ja'nae walks over to Zora's dresser. There's six bottles of perfume, a whole tray of finger-nail polish, and a little dish with gold chains and rings sitting in it. Ja'nae whips out her cotton ball and sprays it with perfume from the red bottle. The room smells like oranges mixed with peppermint. I guess that's better than the coconut-strawberry perfume Ja'nae's been wearing all week. It seems like Ja'nae used up half the bottle.

That's how strong it smells in here.

Zora don't act like she minds Ja'nae messing with her expensive perfume. She's in a good mood today because her mom snuck her sixty bucks. Now she got half of the money she needs to buy the sneakers. But Zora's got her eye on some sixty-dollar jeans now, too. "Daddy already told me I have to contribute forty dollars toward them, and he'll contribute the rest," she says, pulling open her closet door. "When I get my sneakers, I'll have fifteen pairs," she says. All of Zora's sneakers are lined up and organized by color, just like her clothes. "I'll have twenty pairs of jeans when I get my next pair."

We're all eyeballing Zora's stuff. She's got so much, she uses part of her dad's closet and the one in the hallway, too. Two times a year, Dr. Mitchell makes her give some of it away to the Goodwill. But that's no use. Zora's mother just keeps giving her more clothes, or sneaking her money so she can buy more herself.

Mai's got her eye on a red blouse in Zora's closet when, all of a sudden, she says that she's gonna come clean houses with me and Ja'nae. Her dad told her last night that she don't have to work the food truck until him and her can work out their problems. But since she won't be contributing to the family, she'll have to earn her own spending money. "That means lunch money, too," says Mai, "unless I want to bring food from home."

I tell everyone about that cleaning gig Ja'nae's grandmother got us, working for a lady named Miss Baker. Zora says to count her in—the money will come in handy for clothes. Ja'nae and I look away, though, when Zora says she wants in on the kind of money we made last time at Miss Neeta's. Shoot, neither one of us ever told her that we had to give some of it back.

When I say that Miss Baker's place is on Jade Street, Zora changes her tune and says she ain't too sure about going.

"Jade Street's in a rough neighborhood, even worse than Raspberry's," she says.

I know what Zora means. Lots of drugs get sold around there. People be shooting up—and shooting each other.

"Yeah, Jade Street is rough," I say. "But Miss Baker will pick us up and drop us off so we won't be out in the street. And we gonna make two hundred and fifty dollars for cleaning up. That's sixty-two dollars apiece. Good money."

Ja'nae sprays a cotton ball. "Listen, I need the money," she says. "Even if it means we gotta work on Jade Street."

I look at her, and think I shoulda just kept the fifty dollars I took from her after we cleaned Miss Neeta's.

Mai asks why anybody would give all that money for cleaning up. "She could hire a cleaning company for that much cash," she says.

I explain that one of them companies ripped Miss Baker off before. Stole some valuables. "Now she wants to hire kids, 'cause she thinks she can trust us."

Mai and Zora ask how long it's gonna take to make that "good" money.

"It takes as long as it takes," I say, reminding them that they never made that much money at one time before.

• • •

The next day, Miss Baker picks us up in front of the corner store at 5th and Mallow. As soon as we see the car, we know things ain't right. Miss Baker's car is a big blue station wagon that looks like somebody burnt half the paint off with a blowtorch. When we get in it, the engine stops cold.

"All right, Bessy," Miss Baker says. She got a gap between her teeth big enough to hold a slice of bread. "Now don't show off for the girls."

Cars behind us are beeping.

"She can talk all night to this thing. It ain't gonna help," Zora whispers.

But finally Bessy gets going.

My girls ain't saying a word. They're rolling their eyes at me. I'm wondering how Miss Baker's gonna pay us for cleaning when she don't have enough cash to keep her ride running straight.

Miss Baker is a tiny little lady, can't hardly see over the steering wheel. She stays a long time at every stop sign, and she lets other cars pass in front of her.

Jade Street is only twenty minutes away from Mallow, but it takes Miss Baker forty minutes to get there. Once I see the house we'll be cleaning, I'm wishing the car had broke down right outside the store.

That's when Miss Baker explains this ain't the house she lives in. It's a boarding home she owns. "I got ten boarders living here. Me and my daughter run it together."

There's bottles, cans, paper, trash everywhere. Miss Baker says, "You all got your work cut out for you."

I don't want Miss Baker to open the front door. From the yard, I can see some old guy in a wheelchair. He's shoved up to the window in dirty pajamas, drooling spit.

"I feel like I gotta throw up," Zora says.

Ja'nae grabs her hand and holds it tight.

When we get inside, Zora is holding her nose. It smells like pee in here.

One woman is sitting in a wheelchair with socks on her hands, rocking. She's younger than the rest. Miss Baker says that she was in a car accident. She's brown as me, but her skin is ashy, and cracked like she's covered with chalk dust. She's hunched over to one side of the wheelchair, humming.

Zora says, "I'm getting out of here."

The words ain't hardly out of Zora's mouth when some old hunchback man comes up to her and grabs at her jacket. He's so bent over all he can do is stare at the floor. Zora yells for him to stop touching her.

He twists his whole body to the side and looks up at Zora as best he can. "Had my own tailor shop. First black tailor in the city," he says rubbing his fingers together real quick. "Still can spot me some good leather," he says reaching over and touching Zora's coat again. Then he turns his face back to the floor like a child who just got his fingers smacked, and drags his feet up the hall.

Miss Baker tells us we can hang our stuff up in the corner. That there's buckets and rags waiting for us on the second floor. Ja'nae is already doing something we ain't hired to do—wiping dried oatmeal off some old lady's mouth. Talking to her real quiet. Asking her name. Saying she would brush her hair if she wanted.

Zora rolls her eyes. "You have any gloves? Lysol?"

Miss Baker laughs. Shakes her head and laughs some more. "Gloves? Lysol? Where y'all think you at, some hotel? I got buckets, rags, soap, bleach, and water. That's all you need to clean." She moves closer to Zora and looks down at her boots. "And you better do a good job too. The state health inspector is coming in two weeks and things got to be in order, so let's get to work, girls. I ain't paying you to talk."

For starters, there ain't no carpet on the floors and we have to mop them. We each mop one floor apiece. My arms ache. Cleaning up with that cheap stuff Miss Baker gave us makes Mai's fingers swell up and turn red.

"I'm calling my father to tell him about this funky place," Zora says.

"You call and we gonna lose out on all that money," I remind her.

Zora don't argue. She picks up a rag and we all start dusting woodwork.

"Told you to start with the woodwork first. Now we gonna have to sweep the floors again before we leave," Ja'nae says, coming over to me.

"Don't forget the windows," Miss Baker says, inspecting the floors.

She hands us a bunch of newspapers and some vinegar and tells us to be sure not to scratch up her mirrors and windows. There's thirty windowpanes in all. We count every one of them.

Next, Ja'nae yanks off a bedsheet.

"Man," Mai says, holding her nose.

The sheet Ja'nae got in her hand got a big brown stain in the middle.

"She didn't say do the beds. Forget it," I say, trying to grab the sheet from her.

Ja'nae turns and stares at me. Her voice is really low, and sad. "They need someplace clean to sleep."

We all stare at her. There's maybe twelve beds here. And my fingers are like Mai's now. Cracked, red, and itching.

"What if your grandmother lived here?" Ja'nae asks us.

"The nursing home my grandmother lives in has a golf course," Zora says, lifting up her foot and looking at her white leather boot.

There's a long brown mark across the toe.

"Shut up, Zora," I say.

Ja'nae got a good heart. She always wants to do the right thing no matter what.

"Okay, okay," I say. "Ask Miss Baker where the clean sheets are."

Miss Baker bugs us every few minutes, it seems. So before one of us can hunt her down, she comes back to where we are.

"We got more sheets," she says. "Only they in the basement. Dirty. The girl we hired to do the washing quit two weeks ago. Things pile up, you know."

Before we know anything, Ja'nae's volunteering us to wash that stuff. I mean, I don't even wash my own clothes at home. Neither does Zora. But we help Ja'nae peel that stuff off the beds and carry it down to the basement. My whole body smells like pee by the time we done.

"I wanna go. Now," Mai says.

"They don't have nobody else," Ja'nae says, making us feel bad.

I look around. No matter what we do, it's still gonna be a mess in here. But Ja'nae ain't never gonna see that. She's probably thinking about her grandparents. She don't realize that once we gone, this place is gonna look the way it did when we walked in.

"Please," Ja'nae says.

"Okay," I say. "Mai, you stay and do the clothes since your hands are so jacked up. Zora, you go upstairs and wipe down the furniture and pick up a little. That's not so bad, is it?"

Zora gives me this look. "No," she says.

"Ja'nae and me will do the bathrooms."

Everybody's okay with the plan. Only the plan don't work out the way I'm thinking.

CHAPTER EIGHTEEN

Ja'nae's singing and scrubbing out the toilet and tub. Before I'm done washing the windows in the hallway, she's headed to check on the sheets in the washing machine. I figure I can rest up till she comes back. So I sit down on the floor and stretch my legs. I get up a few minutes later and head for the kitchen at the end of the hall.

When I push open the door, there's an old man in there.

"Who you?" he says, like he might hit me if I say the wrong thing.

When I tell him that I'm here to clean, he laughs. Says Miss Baker done found herself another sucker.

"You thirsty?" he asks. I say yes. He leads me to his room, where he points to a refrigerator with a padlock on the front.

"Help yourself," he says, handing me the key. "But I'm watching you," he says, lowering himself onto his bed.

Inside his refrigerator there's bottled water, crackers, and plastic knives and forks sitting on the top shelf right next to cucumbers and cottage cheese. But that ain't what catches my eye. It's the money that makes me lick my lips and swallow more spit than I should. It's stuffed tight in a half-empty bread bag, pushed against a head of rotten lettuce. I can't help but take the bag out to get a better look.

"Come here, gal," the man says, wiping the back of his wrinkled lips with his hand.

He's kind of scary-looking, so I don't hurry over to him. I keep my eyes on the bag of money in my hand.

Soon as I'm close enough, he grabs his money out my hand and says for me to listen up good. "Never spend it. That's the secret. Never spend a penny, if you don't have to."

I look at all that loot, then I look at the old

man again. "Why you put it there?"

The old guy grabs ahold of the rail on the side of the bed. He wraps his hands round it real tight, and pulls. He coughs up some spit and swallows hard. He points to the bag of money. "I been saving for years. I got money stashed in places don't nobody know about. It's all mine, too. And ain't nobody getting it," he says, coughing again and lying back down.

I grab a bottle of water out the fridge. "Here," I say, handing it to him. He starts wiggling his lips, and fanning his hand my way. I go over to him, and put the bottle up to his lips like he's a baby. He balls up his fist and pushes the bottle up so fast, water starts dripping out his mouth and down his neck.

He wipes his mouth with the back of his fist. "Don't go telling about my money, hear?"

I nod my head up and down. And when he starts coughing and spitting again, I start backing out the room.

"Wait," he says. He opens the bag and holds it out to me. "Take some," he says.

I wonder if I'm understanding him right. "Some what?" I say.

"Money, girl. Money," he says, clearing his throat. "Money won't never do you wrong."

I put my hand in the bag and grab as much money as I can. It feels real good in my hands.

"Let me see what you got," he says.

I show him the money.

"That ain't nothing but chump change," he says, laughing, and coughing again. "I still got enough for myself."

"Keep all of it?" I say, figuring I got maybe seventy dollars in my hand.

"Redheaded gals bring you good luck. That's what folks say."

By the end of the day, we're all dead tired. Miss Baker takes us back to Mallow Street in her old clunker. Zora, Mai, and Ja'nae don't say a word to me when we all get out of the car. They are mad because Miss Baker didn't pay us what she promised. Just before she stopped to drop us off, she said she was short of cash. She paid us forty dollars each, not the sixty dollars we was expecting. Zora says this is the last time she will go along with any more of my moneymaking schemes. Mai and Ja'nae agree with her. And not one of 'em even says a word to me for the next thirty minutes we stand there waiting for a bus.

CHAPTER NINETEEN

As soon as I get home, things start falling apart. Momma is standing at the doorway of our building. She's wearing open-toed bedroom slippers.

"Raspberry!" Momma yells, her fist balled up and her thumb pointing toward the door. "Get in this house right now!"

I move past Momma real slow. She don't take her eyes off me for a minute. And I can tell by the way she's looking at me that I got a real hollering coming my way.

When Momma comes inside behind me, she's madder than before.

Momma's hollering, "I work two jobs to keep us from living in the street. And you go and steal money. Why?"

I try to tell Momma I don't know what she's talking about. But she's gone crazy. Walking from room to room yelling at me. Next thing I know, she's in my bedroom, pulling out my money drawers. Emptying my cans of stashed bills from the hole in the wall. Dumping cash all over the place.

"I ain't—didn't—raise no thief."

I'm walking behind Momma. Picking up tens and twenties. Shoving quarters into my pockets. Momma turns around and sees what I'm doing. She grabs my hand, and pulls open my fingers to get the money. "You're *hurting* me," I yell.

But Momma keeps pulling back my fingers. "This is gonna stop here and now," she says, taking the money, and throwing it across the room. "I shoulda made you stop all this money nonsense long before, when I seen how crazy it was making you."

She puts the can down, and goes over to the window. The wind blows the curtains back against the wall.

"Who said I was a thief? Who said I took

their stuff?" I say, taking hold of the can.

"Who said I was a thief? Who said I took their money?" I ask Momma again and again.

Momma tells me that it was Ja'nae's grandfather who said I was a thief. He told Momma that every now and then he sneaks a peek at Ja'nae's diary to see what she's up to. This morning he read something in it about me stealing two hundred dollars of his money.

I'm shaking my head saying that he don't know what he's talking about. I tell Momma that it was Ja'nae who took the money, not me.

Momma looks at me real disappointed like. She turns around and drops a handful of money out the window. I lose it, then. I push her out of my way. I scratch my hand, trying to get at my money. "Momma nooo!" I yell, looking at my money fall to the ground.

Momma is stronger than I am. She takes one hand, pushes me hard, and I end up falling on my butt, and hitting my back against the table. "I guess you gonna stand here and deny taking that fifty dollars from Ja'nae, too," she says, talking about the money I took off Ja'nae's kitchen table.

At first I tell Momma I didn't take it. Then I come clean and say I did but I returned it right away.

She shakes her head and sits for a minute on the windowsill. "I would rather throw it all away, than for you to think it's okay to steal."

There are tears running down Momma's face. She lets loose another fistful of money. "I got a letter from a lawyer today saying that them folks in Pecan Landings don't want us living over there. They think we trash, and you," she says, getting louder, "with all your money-hungry ways, you just prove them right."

Now I see what this is all about. "That money's mine," I say, getting up in Momma's face. I put my hand over hers to make her stop. But even with my hands trying to squeeze hers shut, her fingers uncurl, and my money is gone.

I hear Shoe and other people outside going nuts. "I got me a twenty," he's saying.

"Lord, here come another ten," somebody else says.

I try to tell Momma that this is all a big

mistake. She's so angry about losing the house, she ain't listening to me. She throws the empty can on my bed, and starts grabbing handfuls of loose change from my top dresser drawer. Next thing I know, I hear it bouncing off the pavement. Flying off cars.

For a minute, I don't try to stop Momma anymore. I think that maybe if I act like it don't matter, she will quit. But it's hard for me to act like I don't care.

Momma empties two whole cans of money before she stops. I figure she just gave away two hundred dollars of my cash.

"Check and anybody else out there better give me back my stuff," I yell out the window.

Momma pulls me back inside by my shirt. "I will throw it all out . . . every last penny . . . if you don't get yourself together," she says. She opens her mouth wide to say something else, but closes it when the phone rings. I look at her, and go to answer it.

"The machine will pick it up," she says, holding me back with her arm like a crossing guard does at the light.

I walk over to the window. People are still

waiting for more of my money to fall. Check's got a stick, digging around in the dirt, looking for my stuff.

Momma's got another fistful of my dollars in her hand. She's heading for the window. When I try to trip her, I smack the money out her hand at the same time. She gives me a look that lets me know that she will knock me out, if I keep doing what I'm doing. So I stop, and pray to God that she will cut it out.

When the answering machine picks up, we hear Ja'nae's grandfather's voice. He's apologizing to Momma and me. Saying he talked to Ja'nae about her diary, and she said he misunderstood what she wrote. "It was Ja'nae that took the money out my drawer," he says, sounding embarrassed. "She's the thief, not your girl."

Momma takes a big breath and sits down on my bed.

"I was so upset at not getting the house . . . then Ja'nae's grandfather called about you stealing money. I lost my head, I guess," she says. . . .

She's shaking her head from side to side,

saying she's sorry for throwing my money away. She starts talking to me in words soft and sweet as pudding. I bust out crying when Momma holds me tight. She reminds me again and again that things have a way of turning out, and I know she's right. But deep down inside, I'm still scared. 'Cause without money, you ain't nothing. And people can do anything they want to you.

CHAPTER TWENTY

No sooner than I start cleaning up what's left of my money, Dr. Mitchell comes over. He looks nervous leaving his car on the street with everybody standing around like they're waiting for something more to happen. And before he's inside our place, two kids is sitting on the hood of his ride.

Soon as Momma sees Dr. Mitchell, tears come. She tells him about being turned away from Pecan Landings, and about throwing my money around.

Dr. Mitchell's got his arms around Momma. He's standing in the middle of the room holding her tight, telling her everything will be all right. Momma's crying real hard, and she can't stop. I know it sounds weird, but I feel better, safer with Dr. Mitchell around.

Dr. Mitchell asks me for towels. He wants Momma to lay in her bed and cool down before she makes herself really sick. I'm watching him take care of her. Putting towels in cool water and pressing them on her forehead. Putting on nice music and shutting her bedroom door so she can rest. For once, I'm jealous of Zora.

When Dr. Mitchell offers to help me straighten up the place, I turn him down. But he acts like I ain't said a word. He grabs a broom and starts sweeping up. Then starts talking about how someday things will be better for Momma and me.

"They're just a bunch of triflin' snobs down in Pecan Landings," I snap.

Dr. Mitchell shakes his head and walks over to the window. He plays with the change in his pocket. Taps on the window and tells people to get off his ride. "When things settle down, I'll take your mother to City Hall. We'll talk to people there. File a complaint, if she wants," he says.

Then Dr. Mitchell opens the window, and says, "Now don't make me have to come down there. I said get off my *car*."

I'm tired of not having ever spoken to Dr. Mitchell about his thing with Momma. So, I ask him straight up, "Are you in love with my mom or what?"

I don't cut him no slack. I don't try to help him out by making small talk or changing the subject. I need to know. And he's gonna tell me.

Dr. Mitchell jerks up his pants legs when he goes to sit down. Then he scratches his head, and clears his throat. "I like your mom, Raspberry." That's all he says.

"But you dating her, right?" I ask.

"I like your mother a whole lot. She likes me. But she won't make a solid commitment to me," he says, turning toward me. "Says she's too busy trying to make something out of herself to get fully involved with me."

I'm thinking Momma must be nuts. Turning down a doctor. A smart nice guy with big cash. And her living in the projects, and holding down two jobs.

"So why you all up under her?" I ask.

"Company," he says. "Friendship. Good conversation, I guess." He talks more than he ever did to me before. Telling me about Momma. How smart and strong she is. How determined she is to do something good with her life.

"We have the same values, you know," he says, standing up and getting busy again. "We love our families, work hard, and try to do what's right." His beeper goes off, and he pulls it out of his pocket to check the phone number. "Zora," he says. "I need to give her a call."

While he's in the kitchen on the phone, I get on my hands and knees to pick up more of my money. All I find is ten dollars in change.

Dr. Mitchell says he's gotta be heading home soon, but it's another hour before he goes. He spends some time at Momma's bedside, wiping her forehead with the washcloth. Finally he says good-bye to me. "Take care of your momma. Tell her I'll call her soon," he says.

Momma wakes up as soon as she hears Dr. Mitchell close the front door behind him.

In a little while, she's in the kitchen, pulling out frying pans and making dinner. I don't have no appetite. But I watch her flour up the chicken, melt down the lard, and put the good plates and silverware on the table.

After a while, we're sitting down. But we're not eating the food. Not talking. I'm playing with a string unraveling from Momma's pink tablecloth. Digging in my pocket for the money I made earlier today at Miss Baker's boardinghouse. Thinking about what the old man said to me. "Money won't never do you wrong."

CHAPTER TWENTY-ONE

The first person I see when I jump out Momma's car and walk up the steps to the school is Ja'nae. Me and her already had it out on the telephone about her putting me in her diary. But I believe her when she says her granddad got it all wrong. She's with Ming. I don't have time to play around. So I just say what I mean. "Give me what you owe me," I tell Ja'nae, with my hand out.

"You know Zora ain't speaking to you," she says, walking up the steps with Ming's arm around her shoulder.

"Don't talk to me about Zora. Just give me my money back," I say, matching every step she takes.

Ming looks at me and says that I should chill. Ja'nae asks him to go to her locker and get her science book.

I start to explain to Ja'nae that I'm just about broke, but Ja'nae already knows that. Shoe and Check have been telling everybody about how all my money came pouring out the window.

"Ja'nae," I put my hand out. "Give me back the money I lent you, *now.*"

Ja'nae's shaking her head. Her long, shiny spiral curls pat the sides of her face every time she moves. She tells me that the person who owes her the money ain't paid it back yet.

"Give me the money we made at Miss Baker's—or sell Ming's jacket. Take the jacket to a pawnshop, or sell it on the corner. Do what you gotta, but get my money. Today," I yell.

Ming walks back over to us. Sato's right behind him. Seneca and Kevin are there, too.

I don't want to embarrass Ja'nae and Ming, but I gotta have that money. I can't be walking around broke. So I forget about him and her, and just let him know that I know Ja'nae got him that jacket with money that wasn't hers, and that I want my money back. *Now*.

"You are so lame," Sato says, walking up to me. "Lame and greedy," he says, letting loose a smile so sweet I could just die. "Embarrassing Ming in front of the whole school, busting on your friend, all for a few pennies," he says, shaking his head and walking off.

Don't nobody care Ja'nae owes me two hundred dollars and don't wanna pay up? Don't nobody care that I'm practically broke?

Ming is staring me down. Holding on to Ja'nae's hand tight, and giving me an evil look. "She didn't *buy* me the coat." He's playing with his baby ring.

"I'll tell her," Ja'nae says to him. Then she lowers her voice, and looks me straight in the face. "The coat was Willie's, my cousin who died last year from an asthma attack." Ja'nae looks down at the floor. "Ming didn't want anyone to know," she says even lower, "'cause my cousin had the jacket on when he died."

Ming's looking down at his feet, still

holding tight to Ja'nae's fingers. When he and Ja'nae start to walk off, a white cotton ball falls off her from someplace. She steps on it, and I never do see it again.

"I need my money," I say, following behind her.

"I need my money." Kevin's copying me, getting all up in my business. "Sell some pencils," he says.

"Or rotten chocolate," Seneca says, laughing.

I look at Ja'nae. I want to ask her what happened to the money she took from her granddad. But she's walking off with Ming. Seneca is right with her, looking back at me every once in a while. She's got a smirk on her face. Kevin's got his arms around her shoulders.

They all turn the corner at once. I'm watching 'em go. Watching my money go for good too. I'm standing there, trying to figure out what it's gonna take to get Ja'nae to shake loose my cash, when she comes running back my way. She smells like baby powder and peaches.

"The money," she says, breathing hard.

"The money wasn't for Ming. It was for my mother."

I am tired of Ja'nae and her stories. So I ask her again when she'll be able to pay me. Next thing I know, Ja'nae is digging in her purse. Pulling out dollar bills. Throwing 'em my way.

"You cheap greedy thing," she says, throwing money at me like it ain't nothing. "I told you I didn't have the money. Why couldn't you just leave me be? Why couldn't you just trust me?" she says, still digging in her purse.

I don't wait for kids to do like they did when Momma lost her mind and threw my money out the window. I get down on my hands and knees and stuff the money in my book bag. I stop counting when I get to thirty-five bucks.

"Ja'nae is bugging," I say to Mai when I see her in the hall later on. I tell Mai about the money Ja'nae threw at me.

Mai is walking down the hall, looking at herself in a hand mirror. "Why don't you give

Ja'nae a break?" she asks. "You are just so greedy."

I point my finger in Mai's face and say, "What's that supposed to mean?"

Mai takes a deep breath, and shakes her head. "First you take that fifty from Ja'nae. Then you start harassing her about paying you back."

"What's mine is mine," I say, getting loud.

Mai keeps staring at herself in the mirror. Kevin and Seneca walk by. Kevin says to Mai, "Hey, Karate Kid." Him and Seneca think that's real funny.

Then here comes Sato. He's asking if I got a pencil he can buy. While I'm looking in my bag for one, he says he heard that me and Momma gonna be kicked to the curb. Living on the streets again.

I swallow hard. I wanna say that what he heard is just talk. But I ain't sure. That's why I gotta get the money Ja'nae owes me. Why I gotta figure out a way to replace what Momma threw out the window.

CHAPTER TWENTY-TWO

I got too much on my mind to be a thirteen-year-old. That's what I'm thinking on the bus ride home. So I make a decision. I'm gonna stop thinking about how Ja'nae and me are mad at each other. Stop thinking about the house me and Momma ain't gonna get, and the people who don't want us to live there. I'm gonna forget about Momma and Dr. Mitchell, too. I'm gonna forget everything but filling up my money drawer again, and keeping Momma and me off the streets.

It's nice out today. Don't nobody want to be inside, not even me. So I get off the bus a few blocks early and take my time getting home. The weather done gone crazy.

The temperature shot up to seventy-five even though spring is a ways off. Just like that. It's nice enough for people to be driving around with their hatchbacks up, or sitting out playing cards, and talking trash.

The closer I get to my place, the noisier the world seems. People are talking at the top of their lungs. Laughing like jokes is funnier around here than anywhere else on earth. Blasting their car stereos like they throwing a party and want everybody else to come. But it's all good, 'cause 'round here, there's always somebody to look at, and somebody else's music to listen to.

When I turn the corner, Odd Job, our neighborhood car washer, is doing his thing—making cars shine. Selling frozen Kool-Aid in cups and hawking hand fans that blow water. Soon as I walk up, he tells me to take a frozen icy. But he keeps right on wiping the windshield of somebody's Town Car.

"Raspberry treat!" he shouts, looking my way. "What's shaking, girl?"

I halfway smile at him, and reach my hand inside the cooler for a blue icy. I rub the cool cup on my sweaty forehead, then lick till my tongue turns blue.

Odd Job is quick on his feet. Moving from car to car. Waving one of his guys over to the car that just pulled up. Telling the woman inside she gets a free car wash, 'cause she looking so fine. Odd Job pulls out his money—a roll of bills as fat as a hoagie. When I see all that cash, my mouth starts watering. I lick my lips, and try not to look so greedy.

"Better watch it, Odd Job. Raspberry will take all your dollars," Shoe says, walking up. Shoe reaches into the water cooler and grabs an icy, too.

"You better pay up. I ain't running no credit union," Odd Job says to him.

Shoe slides his hands down into his pants pocket, and comes up with a handful of change.

"I'm paying up today," Shoe says, handing over the money. "How much I owe you?" Shoe's acting like he's grown. Walking with a dip. Fingering the change in his pocket like a man.

"You owe me too much," Odd Job says,

taking the change without counting a dime of it.

"Plenty where that come from. Plenty," Shoe says. He heads across the street to the supermarket. He got the nerve to come back later with a giant-size bag of barbecue chips. And swearing he ain't sharing them with nobody. I want to punch him in the face. I know it's my money he's spending.

Odd Job's working hard. He got sweat dripping down the side of his face, and soaking the top of his pants, right underneath where the belt is. But he don't stop moving. He keeps washing them cars. I'm sitting here, watching him. My tongue is blue from the icy that dribbled down the front of my shirt. I can't help but wonder how much money he makes in a day.

Odd Job must have read my mind. "You here to make some money?" he asks.

"I could use a few pennies in my pocket," I say, remembering how I used to help him out when Momma and me first moved around here.

Odd Job throws me a wet rag. I scrub

windows clean with vinegar and water. Hustling hand fans right along with him.

By the time I finish, it's dark out. And I know I'm in trouble 'cause I missed my curfew.

On the way home, I count my money five times. I figure I can double it if I buy up pencils from the dollar store and sell 'em for twenty-five cents each. So I go to the dollar store and buy a whole bunch of pencils.

When I get home, Shoe's grandma lays me out as soon as I put my key in the door. "Raspberry. Your mother's going crazy calling around looking for you," she says, leaning over in her wheelchair and hollering downstairs at me. "And look at you. Just look," she says, frowning up her face and shaking a head full of curlers.

I look down at my chest. My white shirt has got fat black smudges on it, from me leaning against those dirty cars.

"Your momma is worried sick about you," she says. "She got her hands full enough, and you ain't making things no easier for her, you wild, selfish thing." She starts backing her wheelchair into her apartment. I can hear the wheels squeaking. "Selfish, selfish, selfish. That's what you is," she says, slamming the door behind her.

CHAPTER TWENTY-THREE

Today, Odd Job is talking my ears off. Working me hard, too. By the time it's dark, I got thirty dollars in my pocket, including what I made at school selling more pencils. My arms ache so bad I can hardly pick up my backpack.

The ten-minute walk from Odd Job's corner to home seems like a hour. It's getting nicer out every day. And everybody and their mother is out here, including Shoe, whose grandmother is hollering out the window for him to get in the house. He's sitting on the chair Momma left in the street to hold her parking spot. There's a bunch of boys, including Check, out there with him. One of them tries to trip me when I go by. "Punk," I say, rolling my eyes at him. Then getting real smart I ask them why they gotta be sitting in front of our door making it hard for people to get inside. Check tells me to be quiet. Shoe throws an empty pop bottle my way. Their grandmother is still yelling for them to come inside the house.

When I step inside the building, the hallway is pitch-black. The lightbulb is out. I hold the door open with my book bag, so the streetlight will help me see better. I look back at Shoe and Check. I can see in their faces that they don't care. I doubt they'd even pee on me if I was on fire.

I drag my hands across the hallway walls, trying to feel my way to our front door. I'm walking slow. Looking all around me. Wondering if somebody is hiding behind the steps, or by the door. Swallowing hard when I see that our front door ain't locked, like when I left home. It's open. And it's pitch-black in there.

I cut on the light and push the door open wider. I call for Momma, thinking maybe she came home early. A funny noise comes out my mouth when I get inside and see what I see. Our couch is gone. The microwave is gone, and so is the television.

I'm smart enough not to go any further. I back out the door, and run upstairs to Check's grandmother's place to call the police. Momma shows up before they come. She goes through the apartment holding my hand. "I can't believe this," she says.

I pry her fingers loose and run back to check on my stash. I open the drawer and see the cans turned over every which way— empty. I look under the mattress, but they got the rest of it. Every last penny. Slowly, I go back to the other room where Momma is sitting on the floor.

Momma always knows what to do. But she's sitting here now, crying with me, saying she don't know if she can go on no more. And I don't, either. "I—I keep trying to hold on. To be strong. But I'm tired, Lord!" she yells. She goes to the window and pulls it wide open. "I'm tired!" she's screaming. "Sick and tired!"

I go to Momma and put my head on her chest. We hold each other. And we both make the same sounds when we cry; like a tired baby that's been crying a long time, because nobody cared enough to come see about it.

Momma wipes both our faces and sits on the windowsill. Check and Shoe are still out there. So are lots of other people. They're playing craps. Bunched up on steps in front of the boarded-up place across the way. Some girl is jiggling her butt to music coming from a car parked on the pavement. Three boys circle around her, and they take turns trying to outdance her.

"Somebody out there got our stuff, Raspberry," Momma says, sounding mad now. Walking over to the cabinets. Pulling 'em open two at a time. She grabs boxes of cereal, bags of rice, plastic ketchup packets—anything she can get her hands on.

"You shoulda just took it all," she says, going over to the window and throwing our food. She leans herself out the window and screams louder than anything, "You shoulda took everything!"

I hear people outside cursing. Saying we better not come down there if we know what's good for us. I sit at the table thinking that Momma is just making it worse and worse.

She goes over to the front door and props a kitchen chair under the doorknob. "We can't stay here no more," she says. "Even if we get the locks fixed, they will come back again. We—we're sitting ducks now."

I tell her that we can't let people run us off. But she says we can't stay now that our place's been hit. "And you here always alone. Sooner or later, something really bad will happen."

Check and Shoe are still outside. I see Shoe pointing at our window when I go over to pull the shade down.

"We gotta travel light, like before," Momma says, fingering a broken plate. "Just a few things. Only what we need."

I look at her like she's crazy. "Like before?" I say, feeling my heart speed up.

She turns my way, and holds my face in her hands. "Just come with me."

"We going back to the streets?" I say, reaching into my pocket for my stash.

"Not me," I yell, walking around the room. "Not me. I got money," I say, pulling dollars and change out my pocket. "See?" I say, pushing the money in her face. Momma pushes my hand out the way.

"We're lucky. Spring is on the way. A few blankets to keep the evening chill off of us, and we'll be okay," she says, going to her bedroom, stuffing pants and work clothes in a green plastic bag. Not seeing, until it's too late, me standing there wetting myself like a baby.

Momma peels off my wet pants, hands me a towel, and tells me to throw everything in the plastic trash bag. "I'll hand wash them before we go."

"Go where?" I ask, while she pulls my shirt over my head, almost pulling my face off, too.

Momma doesn't answer. She bends down, and tells me to lift my foot up. She takes my socks off, and stuffs all the clothes into the bag.

"Why can't we stay with somebody for a while? Maybe Ja'nae, Mai, or Zora."

She shakes her head. Sticks her hand inside the shower and turns on the hot water. "Don't you remember what it was like before?" Momma asks. "People getting mad 'cause we ate too much of their food. Dropping hints that they wanted us out their place."

I look at my leg. There's a trail of pee from my thigh to my ankle. I rub it with my hand at first. Grab a wet rag and rub it till my skin stings.

"I ain't living on the streets no more," I say, feeling like I gotta pee on myself all over again. "I'll do foster care before I do that."

Momma's eyes let me know that she didn't like what I just said to her. But her voice is still warm and soft, like the steam filling up the bathroom and fogging up the mirror. She pulls back the shower curtain, and hands me the soap. "*I* can take care of you," she says, when I step into the shower.

Before I close the curtain, I ask why we can't stay in a hotel.

"We gotta save money," Momma says.

"I *got* money," I say jumping out the

shower, running to my room to dig in my pants pocket. I run back to the bathroom, with money balled up in my hand. "Here. Here's a hundred and fifty dollars. We can stay someplace nice for a while," I say, giving Momma my money.

Momma smiles at the money in her hand. She pulls back the shower curtain and says for me to get inside. "We better hold on to this," she says, pulling the curtain closed behind me. "We don't know what the day will bring."

"This is all your fault!" I scream. "You threw away my money . . . made them come after us," I say, feeling the steam. "You're the reason we had to live in the streets the *first* time," I cry. "If it wasn't for you, we would still have our own place. Not be living in the projects and in the streets and being scared of doing without."

I know it ain't true, some of the things I'm saying. But I can't stop the words, or the tears. So for ten more minutes I yell and scream and cry and tell Momma that I ain't never gonna be like her when I grow up. I'm gonna have money. I'm gonna take care of my children. I'm gonna keep them safe.

It don't take no time for the water to go cold, and for the steam to disappear from the bathroom. When I step out the shower, Momma is there. Helping to wipe me down. Reminding me to brush my teeth. Telling me everything will be all right.

On the news, they call it breaking and entering. But I don't remind my mother of that. She already knows that what we're doing is wrong. I watch out for the neighbors when Momma takes a screwdriver and breaks out the glass window to the kitchen door at the house in Pecan Landings.

It's the middle of the night. We got a key-chain flashlight shining on the floor in front of our feet, so we can see where we're going. I'm holding Momma's arm tight. We drop our bags. Get on our knees to dig pillows and a blanket out one of the biggest of the bags. Momma covers me up and kisses me good night. She's snoring almost as soon as she rolls over, taking most of the cover with her.

I can't sleep. I try, but it's too quiet.

At night, I'm used to hearing radios thumping, dogs fighting, or somebody cussing somebody out. But here in Pecan Landings, it's like everything is dead. I get up and crawl over to the window to look outside. Nobody is hanging out on the street corners, or sitting out on their front steps. Nothing is moving.

I go back over to Momma, and tell her to give me some of the covers. She sits up, quick. Looks around like she don't know where she is. Shakes her head and smiles at me. She lays back down, pulling some of the cover off her and putting it onto me. "Go to sleep," she says, putting her arm around me. I close my eyes, and I'm back on the streets again. Dreaming that same old dream. I'm too tired to wake myself up. So I push the cart. All night long, I push the cart.

CHAPTER TWENTY-FOUR

Momma's shaking me. Trying to get me up, so we can leave this place before people start heading for work. I turn back over. I know Momma's gotta go to work. I feel like I been working all night long myself. I open my eyes to ask Momma to please let me sleep a little longer. She's got dark circles under her eyes. Her smile is gone. She is tired. Too tired to argue with me this morning.

But she still doesn't give in. She says she's gotta get our car out of the driveway or people will suspect something. And even though it's still dark out, she tells me to hurry up and get dressed. "It's bad enough that we're here without permission. If someone finds you here alone, we'll be in more trouble than you know."

Before too long, we are sneaking out the back door, and driving away. Momma and me eat breakfast at a tiny restaurant with real nice dishes and the best doughnuts I ever had. After that, she drops me off in front of school. It's early. Nobody is around except a few teachers going into the building. Momma says that she needs to take care of some business before work. She drives away without even saying good-bye.

For a minute, I try to talk myself out of skipping school. But the next thing I know, I'm walking across the street, waiting for a bus. I figure, I need the money more than I need to hear teachers run off at the mouth today. So I go to Odd Job's where I know I can make some fast bucks without being hassled.

Odd Job don't take no breaks. Him and his boys are right here on the corner making dough from the lunchtime crowd. He throws me a rag soon as I walk up. Don't even ask me why I ain't in school.

I'm getting good at washing cars and making change. Odd Job saying maybe he just gonna let me handle the money. "You do figuring faster than anybody I know," he says, taking a rag and wiping some dirt out my hair.

When it slows down, he finally asks me, "Why ain't you in school?"

His boys is working on the other cars. He's sitting in a lounge chair. Got the seat back and the footrest up. I'm sitting on a metal milk crate. I tell him I just didn't want to go to school today.

Odd Job sits up. Pushes the footrest back, and stares at me good. "Don't lie," he says, his voice getting serious.

It's like being with the principal or something. Only Odd Job ain't got on no suit, and he probably ain't sat at a desk since he dropped out of high school.

"You can't lie if you gonna be working with me," he says, standing up, yelling at some man across the way. He laughs. "You want your car washed? I'm open more days than 7-Eleven," he says to the man. Then he turns to me, and tells me that he knows what went down at our house. Starts saying how Check and Shoe hooked up with some baby thugs and they all went in our place and got busy.

My fists curl up. "Where they at?" I say.

"You gonna do something to them?" Odd Job says, taking a bunch of clean rags off the fence. "You a fighter now?"

I feel my fist relax. "He got our stuff."

"Your stuff is gone. It's all over the place."

"They know where it's at," I say, walking up to a car and asking if they want to buy something to drink. Washing their front window before they even ask. When I get back to Odd Job he acts like we wasn't having no conversation. He got his lounge chair laying back and his eyes closed. Before too long, he's snoring. People are walking by him to catch the bus and go to work. They're driving up to get a wash or something to drink. And he's asleep.

His boys, they don't miss a beat, though. They're wetting down rides. Pushing those fans. Telling me to hustle if I wanna hold on to the change bag. Next thing I know, Odd Job is closing up the lounge chair. Standing up and stretching. Starting the conversation right where he left off ten minutes ago.

"It's water under the bridge," he says, talking about our stolen stuff.

"You would take care of Check and Shoe if they stole your stuff. I know it," I say, taking out a pink lemonade icy and licking it.

"I don't lend money, and I don't make no enemies," he says. "And when people screw me, I let natural consequences take care of 'em."

I look at Odd Job real funny like. He walks away, and starts working on somebody's ride. When he comes back, he says, "You don't have to shoot people, or hurt them, when they mess with your head and stuff. Just give 'em time. They gonna do something to make they own lives miserable."

I still don't get what he's saying. He can see that on my face.

"Natural consequences, Raspberry Cherry. Just leave people be for long enough, and they will screw things up for themselves, sure 'nuff."

I ain't sure if Odd Job got no family or

nothing. But every once in a while, somebody like me, a kid, be working for him. And every now and then, I hear about somebody taking off with some of his cash. The word on the street is things happen when you cross him. Natural consequences? I ain't so sure.

"Where you and your Momma staying?" he asks.

I give him a look that says I don't have a clue.

"I got a place," he says. "It ain't much. Last time I looked, the dogs did it up real bad. But it'll keep you warm. Got running water and a little furniture."

I look at Odd Job. He got on these funny boots. They wrapped with tape right across the middle. And the shoestrings are missing. His pants are drooping, and he gotta pull 'em up every once in a while. But the word around here is that he got money. Lots of it. Property, too. Apartments all around this way.

"I gotta talk to Momma," I say. "Maybe she's planning on us coming back home tonight."

Odd Job shakes his head. "I wouldn't. You

on the list now. Folks gonna be busting in all the time."

I been out here a while. I smell like it, too. So when another car pulls up, I stay put. Let Odd Job's boys go for it.

"I ain't sure where you gonna be laying your head, you know," he says, handing me another icy. "But you better not be missing no more school. You hear?" he says.

I see in his eyes that he means what he's saying. "I'm going to school tomorrow," I say.

"I know. I know, Miss Raspberry Sweets," he says, squirting me with one of them water fans. Then he tells me to get busy, and stop costing him money by eating up his profits. Before I know anything, he's handing me a bottle of water, and telling me to take a break, and go use the bathroom at the gas station three blocks away. "Girls shouldn't be smelling like men. You know what I mean?" he says.

I take the hint, and go get myself cleaned up. When I get back, I grab me a rag and start washing down the first car I see.

"Raspberry! What in the world?"

It's Zora's dad, Dr. Mitchell. And I can tell by his voice, he ain't happy about finding me out here like this.

CHAPTER TWENTY-FIVE

"Hey, Dr. Mitchell," I say, rubbing a spot off the hood. "You getting the whole thing done, or just the windows?" I don't look him in the eyes.

"Are you cutting school?" he says, stepping out of his car.

I find another tiny spot and start rubbing that one, too.

"Get in," he says, going around to the other side, opening the door for me. "What's going on? Look at yourself," he says, making a face.

I look at Odd Job. Then I look at Dr. Mitchell. "I ain't finished."

"Let's go. *Now!*" he says.

He's acting like my father or something. Bossing me around. But I do what he says, 'cause all he gotta do is tell Momma, and then I'm gonna be in more trouble.

"I gotta go, Odd Job," I say, handing over the money pack.

He reaches in the purple sack and pulls out some bills. He hands me fifteen dollars and says he'll see me later. "After school one day, all right?"

When I'm in Dr. Mitchell's car, I hear Odd Job's big voice say for us to hold up. "Raspberry Cherry," he says, leaning inside the car. "You cool for tonight?" he asks, trying to see if I got a warm place to lay my head.

"Yeah."

"'Cause you know I got a place for y'all," he says to me, real quiet. "Except for that dog crap, it's all right. You know," he says.

"I know," I say.

Next thing I know, Dr. Mitchell's driving off. Turning on some corny music from the station that only plays stuff with violins and flutes.

"Okay. Let's talk," he says. "I can't reach

your mother. You're out here when you should be in school. And now Odd Job's saying he has a place for you two to live."

We make it to the next corner before he takes his hand and slaps it on the dashboard. "What's going on with you two? Is your mother all right?"

Before he can ask me anything else, the tears come. "We, we gonna be living back on the streets again," I say, in a shaky voice. I got my money in my hand and I'm shaking all over. Crying so much that Dr. Mitchell pulls the car over on the side of a busy street and holds me till I stop.

"Why didn't she call me?" he says, wiping my face with a tissue. "You could have stayed with us."

I look at him, and start crying again. "You don't know, Dr. Mitchell," I say. "When you ain't got your own place, people don't treat you right. They say come stay with us, but when you do, they act like they can't wait for you to leave."

"You think it's better to be on the streets?" he says. "To sleep on floors or out in the cold?"

I don't know how many tears a person got inside 'em, but it must me a whole lot, 'cause for the next hour, I cry. My face is red, my eyes are puffed, and my nose is raw from rubbing it. Dr. Mitchell ain't got no more tissues left when I'm done.

"Darn it," he says, slamming his fist on the steering wheel, and cutting on the engine. "I forgot to pick up Zora. She probably took the bus by now," he says, reminding me that school let out early today.

We race through red lights and almost have an accident trying to get to Zora. On the way, Dr. Mitchell says he wants us to stay with them. "I'll pick your mother up from work tonight and bring her home. She needs to learn she can depend on people," he says, pulling up to the school. Seneca is sitting out front. She says that Zora left a while ago.

By the time we get to their house, Zora is unlocking the front door. She rolls her eyes at me when I step out the car. Her father kisses her, and apologizes for not picking her up. But he don't tell her why he's late. Or why he got me with him. He just says that me and

Momma will be staying with them for a while.

Zora don't like it when people spring surprises on her. She don't look at me or say a word.

When we get upstairs, Zora says, "I need privacy." Then she shuts her bedroom door in my face.

CHAPTER TWENTY-SIX

At Dr. Mitchell's, Momma sleeps on the couch. I sleep on the floor in a sleeping bag in Zora's room, but she ignores me all night. During the car ride to school the next day, she keeps her mouth shut and her lips pocked out. Her dad tells her to apologize to me for being so rude. She never does, though. When the car stops, she hops out and runs into the building. I see now why Momma doesn't want to live with anybody else. It's bad enough not having a house, let alone being treated like you ain't wanted by people who are supposed to be your friends.

I don't have time to feel sorry for myself, though. As soon as I get out of Dr. Mitchell's car, Sato is up in my face. "Ja'nae's in there with the cops," he says, grabbing me by the arm and almost dragging me up the steps to the building.

"What?" I say, pulling my arm away from him.

He points to a squad car parked in front of the building. "Yeah, the police. They got her in the principal's office right now," Sato says, tugging on his skullcap.

I forget that me and Ja'nae ain't speaking. I hurry inside and go straight to the principal's office. There's a big cop standing out front. Another one inside by the school counselor's office, where Ja'nae is sitting.

"They can't make you live with people you don't want to. Can they?" she's saying.

The police officer tells me to stay back, unless I got other business here. A lady cop tells Ja'nae that her grandparents have custody of her, and that her mom cannot just walk in here demanding her school records so she can take her to California to live.

Ja'nae smells like orange blossoms today. When I get close, I see that she's crying and holding some woman's hand. She's kind of pretty. Got long braids with cowrie shells in them. Silver bracelets from her wrist to her elbow. She's skinny, too. She's telling Ja'nae that everything will turn out okay.

"But I *want* to live with her," Ja'nae tells the cop. "She's got money. She can take care of me," she says, pulling money out of her pocket. That's when I realize the woman is Ja'nae's mom, the Heifer.

"This isn't about money, girl," the cop says, looking down at her. "Your grandparents got custody. If this woman wants you to come live with her, she needs to take it to court," he says, pointing to Ja'nae's mom.

Ja'nae's granddad walks in. He's cursing at the cops, and threatening to have Ja'nae's mom locked up if she don't get herself back on the first bus out of town.

While the cops push him into one of the guidance counselor's offices, I sneak over to Ja'nae. "You okay?" I ask.

She nods yes. Then she introduces me to her mother. We can hear Ja'nae's granddad from the back office. He's telling all of Ja'nae's business. Saying how when she was three her mom took off and left her alone in the house for two days. Then he says how her mother would spend all the money on foolishness and not have no food in the house. "That's why I chased her off six years ago," he's telling the police. "Why I didn't want her back in that child's life."

I'm wondering if Ja'nae knew any of this before. She ain't letting on that she does. And her mom don't seem bothered by her granddad's words. She's just sitting there, not letting go of Ja'nae's hand. Staring at the white wall in front of her.

The principal tells me to get out. At first, I start to walk away. Then I hear Ja'nae crying again. Saying that nobody got the right to separate her from her mom no more. I don't care that the cop has got his hand on my arm, or that the other cop ain't talking so nice to me no more. I grab a hold of Ja'nae, and squeeze her tight. "We still girls," I say.

"You're looking at a suspension, Miss Hill, if you don't make your way out of here right now," the principal says.

Ja'nae begs the principal to let me stay. Her granddad is yelling again, so the principal tells me to shut up and sit down so that he can quiet Ja'nae's granddad. Kids are piling in the office wanting to hear what's going on. The bell is ringing and a teacher is getting ready to make morning announcements. The office is small. It's like a zoo in here.

"What the devil's going on here?" one cop says. "Can't you control your own school?" he yells at the principal when Ming walks in asking to see Ja'nae.

"If this doesn't concern you, get out!" the principal snaps. He takes Ming by the arm and leads him out the office.

"Ming!" Ja'nae yells.

"That's it, everybody out," the principal says, coming over to us. He takes me by the arm, drags me over to the door, and says, "To class, Miss Hill." Then he shuts the door in my face.

CHAPTER TWENTY-SEVEN

When school's out, I don't even know where I'm supposed to go. Momma ain't called me all day. When I tried to reach her at work, they said she wasn't there. I'm sitting on the school steps trying to figure out if I should go to the house in Pecan Landings, or back to our old spot. It's nice out, so I don't rush. I just sit. I don't even say nothing when Seneca walks by making smart remarks about me not having a bed to sleep in. When Sato comes up, I'm ready to cry my eyes out for the second time this week.

Sato sits down next to me. One of his pant legs is pushed up to his knee. He's wearing a T-shirt and carrying his jacket across his arm.

Sato sits by me for a long time not talking. Just watching people walking by. He ain't got on no socks, and his sneakers is untied. He plays with the string, when he ain't checking folks out. I want to ask what he's waiting for. But it's so nice having him here, and us not picking on each other. So we just sit.

"You scared?" he asks me.

At first I try to think of something smart to say to him. But he seems like he means what he's asking me. So I come clean. "Yeah."

He pulls off a sneaker and wiggles his long toes. "You got a place to stay, right?"

I shake my head up and down, knowing full well that I ain't so sure.

He puts on his sneaker and makes like he ready to leave. "You know that stuff I said about you being a troll living under the bridge?"

"Yeah."

"I was just being smart."

"I know."

"Sometimes, though, you just get on my last nerve with all your money talk." Then, he stares at me so hard, I turn away. "Well, I guess it's better to have a cute girl get on your nerves than a ugly one," he says, pulling on my bushy ponytail.

I swallow hard, and stare at him, too. "You are *sooo* good-looking," I want to say. But all I do is smile, and wonder if one day him and me will get together or something.

Sato walks down the steps backward, looking at me, and playing with his earring at the same time. "Ja'nae going to live with her mom?" he asks, changing the subject.

I scratch my head. "I don't know," I say. I saw Ja'nae just before her granddad made her go home. "She finally came clean about why she took her granddad's money, and couldn't pay me what she owed me. She used the money to pay her mother's bus fare here. They been planning this a long time, I guess."

Sato shakes his head. "Her mother ain't gonna stick around nohow."

I put my hand in front of my face to block the sun. "How you know?"

"I know. That kind of mother don't never stay put long. You waiting on your mom?" Sato asks.

"Yeah," I lie. Truth is, I don't know what I'm waiting for. I'm just waiting.

Sato smiles and pulls some rolled-up papers out his back pocket. Then he waves, and starts walking away.

"You late, Miz Hill," I hear him say. I think he's kidding around at first and don't even look up till Momma opens her door and starts in on him.

"Boy, what you doing out here dressed like some hoodlum?" she says, fanning for me to come on.

"I'm styling, Miz Hill," he says, turning around in a circle so she can see every part of him. "You could be styling too if you turned your ride in for a *real* car."

Sato walks over to the car like it's *his* mother who came to pick him up. Momma's eyeing me. When I'm inside the car, she reaches over and gives me a hug. Hands me a six-pack of gum. I offer Sato a stick before Momma drives away. Of course, he says he wants two pieces, not one.

For the first time that I can remember, I'm glad to see Momma's beat-up car. And I don't even say nothing smart when the mirror falls off at the first red light we get to.

She tells me she's been on the phone talking to the city. Still trying to get us into the new place in Pecan Landings.

"But where we gonna live now?" I ask.

Momma reaches her hand out for a stick of gum. She's quiet, like she's thinking.

I'm back to crying again. Momma starts looking around the car for tissues. I dig in my pockets and book bag. Pull out some tissues, and a few dollars come flying out, too. I see a five- and a ten-dollar bill. The money I got from Odd Job. Then I remember his offer. "Odd Job's got a place we can use," I tell Momma. She sits there a minute.

"I ain't getting excited," she says, starting the engine. "But it's a place to lay our heads," she says, pulling off.

I got my fingers crossed. The way things are going, I ain't so sure things with Odd Job gonna work out. But I hope they do. I sure hope they do.

CHAPTER TWENTY-EIGHT

Momma drives to see Odd Job's place. She says she wants to check it out before she decides if we gonna stay. We ain't got no place to live and she's wanting to see if the apartment in the building Odd Job owns is good enough for us. Seems to me, if she thought the streets was good enough once, she can't complain about a place with a little dog poop in it.

"It ain't that the place can't be fixed up," Momma says, when we're finished looking around Odd Job's spot. "It's just that it's gonna take a while."

Odd Job owns his house. But it's run-down and it smells bad.

I go in the bedroom, open the window up

wide, and stick my head out so I can clear the stink out my nose.

"Maybe we'll stay here for tonight, then move on," Momma says.

"Can't we stay in a hotel?"

Momma sits in a chair, and hangs her head down. "We don't really know what life is gonna throw our way, Raspberry," she says. "But we shouldn't be wasting our time or money on no hotel."

I look Momma's way. I think about all that money she threw away. Think about us living in the streets and maybe heading right back there again. I want to tell Momma that I'm tired of living like this. But then I see her pulling at the nasty carpet in the living room. Saying how she thinks the floor underneath might be in good shape. Talking about painting the kitchen, and going to the dollar store to buy some new curtains. I dig in my pocket, and hold tight to the little bit of money I got left. Tears come to my eyes when I think how hard I worked to get my money, and how fast it was gone. "At least I got Momma," I say, looking out the window.

"No matter what, I still got her."

Momma and me work our fingers to the bone trying to make that apartment look like something. But it still ain't ready for us to move into yet. For once though, Momma puts her pride aside and calls Dr. Mitchell. She asks if I can stay the night at his place. She's gonna stay behind and clean up here some more. Dr. Mitchell knows better than to argue with Momma. So when he comes by he stays a while and helps out too. Even brings us some chicken and fries to snack on.

On the ride to his place, Dr. Mitchell and me don't say much. Me, I'm thinking about Zora and how she treated me after I stayed at their place the last time. I got my fingers crossed, hoping she don't act like that no more.

Soon as I see Zora, I know we're tight again. She hands me a pair of pajamas. Says that we can do each other's nails after I shower, if I want. She and me stay up late talking about what happened to Ja'nae at school today. Then Zora apologizes for treating me so mean. "We girls," she says, "we gotta stick together no matter what."

I like to sleep in on Saturday mornings. Zora does too. But after Dr. Mitchell wakes us up to say that he's headed out to take care of some business, me and Zora get up and make some breakfast. Then we head for Ja'nae's place.

We knock at Ja'nae's door for a long time. Don't nobody answer. I know somebody's home, though. I can hear Ja'nae's grandfather's big mouth through the basement window. I sit down on the front steps, thinking on what to do. Then Zora and me go to the side of the house where Ja'nae's room is and throw some small stones at the window until Ja'nae appears.

"My momma took off again. She said there's too much drama here." When I look closer, I can see that Ja'nae's been crying. "My granddad is holding me prisoner until he is sure Momma's out of town for good."

Ja'nae is talking low.

"How's Ming? Tell him I miss him."

"I will," I say.

It's quiet for a minute. Ja'nae throws something out of the window. "Give this to Ming," she says. It's a crumpled-up piece of paper with bunches of cotton balls inside. They smell like cherries.

"Tell Ming to carry one in his pocket every day till he sees me again."

Ja'nae's leaning out the window. "I gotta go," she says, before her granddad yells her name, pulls her away from the window and slams it shut.

When we get back to Zora's house, Momma's car is out front. So is Dr. Mitchell's.

Momma gets out of the car and gives me a hug.

"You been painting?" I ask, looking at the yellow paint on her shoes.

"After you all left," she says, waving bye to Zora when she goes inside the house, "Odd Job came by to check on things. He had a can of paint, and helped me put the first coat on."

Momma looks tired. There are circles around her eyes.

"I been up half the night, worrying. Trying to figure out if I'm doing right by you," she says, telling me to get in the car. She's pulling out the parking space before she even says where we're headed. Next thing I know, she's pulling up to the place at Pecan Landings.

She turns and faces me. "We got a good chance of moving in here, you know."

I look at her like she's crazy.

"This morning Dr. Mitchell took me to see a lawyer friend of his. The lawyer, Mrs. Bloom, says she knows the folks in Pecan Landings want to prevent the city and the landlord from letting us move here since we would be on Section Eight. She says she'll go to court to fight for us to be able to move in this here house, if that's what I want."

I ask Momma how we can afford to hire a lawyer. She smiles. Then she tells me that since Mrs. Bloom knows we don't have a lot of money, she will let Momma pay her a little at a time.

I am so happy, I could just scream. Momma feels the same way, I guess. She's squeezing me so hard I feel like she's gonna snap me in two.

"It won't happen right away," she says. "But by summer's end, I bet we'll be able to call this place home."

We both get out of the car and stand in front of the house. Momma leans her face in her hands and rubs her eyes with her palms. I rub circles on her shoulder bones. I press my thumbs into her tight neck muscles. Listen to her say how good that feels. She closes her eyes for a minute. Then her back arches up and her arms stretch up toward the sky.

"We're going to have to paint this here place, too," she says, walking up the front porch steps. "Dr. Mitchell says he'll lend a hand."

"I bet Ja'nae and 'em will too," I say, following behind her.

"I think peach would be a pretty color for the living room and dining room," Momma says, closing her eyes and taking in the warm afternoon breeze. "What color room do you want?" she asks.

"Blue," I tell her. "With stars on the ceiling."